PRAISE FOR
CAREER BREAKTHROUGH PLAYBOOK:
GET UNSTUCK, GET AHEAD

"*Career Breakthrough Playbook* is like having a team of mentors by your side—offering real-life examples, emotional intelligence tools, and practical strategies for every stage of life. Whether you're a student, parent, or professional, this isn't just a guide—it's a lifelong growth companion."

— **Nidhi Mithil Bhandare**,
director at MindLancer, parenting & career coach, author

"Finally, a tremendous and timely gift for each of us here in the field, doing the work. The authors have encapsulated the essence of leadership and synthesized the steps, processes, blind spots to be aware of, preparation needed, and execution paramount to advance up the ladder and provide mission-critical leadership as we work with tireless passion and meaning to improve our organizations from within. The daily disciplines of leadership, now mapped as a guide for sustainable advancement in support of our collective quests for palpable end-to-end improvement at scale along the continuum of servant-leadership in both public and private organizations. This book adds to the canon at a critical inflection point in our history. Magnificent!"

— **Matthew H. Malone, Ph.D.**,
former urban superintendent of schools and
former secretary of education for the
Commonwealth of Massachusetts

"This playbook is truly one of a kind. The authors' perspectives on career paths are compelling and deeply relatable. Their stories, strategies, and resources equip readers with the tools to stay motivated, pursue growth, and take charge of their careers. It's a must-read for anyone seeking employment, considering a career change, climbing the ladder, or looking to enhance their leadership skills."

— **Ms. Maria Lita Sarmiento, MBA**,
career and employment manager
at Hudson County Community College

"This book is a timely, practical guide for navigating the changing landscape of the future of work. Covering career planning, communication, networking, emotional intelligence, and leadership, it reflects the World Economic Forum's call for reskilling and lifelong learning—especially in the current digital and AI era. This book will equip you with essential tools and skills to thrive in this new world of work."

— **Dr. Vincent Ong**,
professor of business education at
Regent's University London

"*Career Breakthrough Playbook* is a powerful resource co-authored by six brilliant experts who bring clarity, simplicity, and actionable insight to the six critical skills every professional needs to grow. What sets this book apart is its ability to offer more than just strategies—it gives readers something far more valuable: hope. This playbook is both a guide and a companion for anyone ready to take their next bold step."

— **Robert J. Hunt**,
executive leadership coach at REF Dallas

"Reading this book felt like a conversation with experienced peers who understand what it means to lead, evolve, and stay true to oneself under pressure. It's a relevant guide for professionals navigating demanding roles in complex environments. It offers grounded wisdom and actionable tools that resonate with the realities of leadership today. I see it as a companion for anyone looking to grow with intention, lead with impact, and remain anchored through pressure and change."

—Alaa Demnati,
head of ICMPD Jordan and Lebanon

"This book provides a meaningful roadmap for professionals who are navigating complexity and questioning how to grow without losing themselves. It's a practical and deeply human guide that reminds us: you are not alone, and you can rise—without burning out."

— Souhaieb Khayati,
head of the Danish Institute for Human Rights,
Tunisia office

"*Career Breakthrough Playbook* is a masterfully curated guide that speaks directly to professionals seeking clarity, confidence, and momentum in their careers. Each chapter blends expert knowledge with relatable experiences, making this more than just a book—it's a career companion. Highly recommended for anyone preparing for their next big leap."

— Jigna Malwankar,
founder of Bookoholics Book Club
and IT professional

"This book is a great, practical read that gives tools anyone can follow for career success. I really like how it incorporates emotional intelligence—an extremely important aspect of good leadership, yet often overlooked in discussions about career success. I like how you explain emotional intelligence in an easy-to-understand way for a wide audience, highlighting its growing importance for companies, contradicting the very relevant current concern many people have of AI taking jobs."

— **Sofia Chantit**,
CEO and co-founder of The American Selections.com,
co-founder of Isness Enterprises Influencer

"*Career Breakthrough Playbook: Get Ahead, Get Unstuck* is the ultimate guide for professionals who are ready to take control of their career trajectory with clarity, confidence, and purpose. The collaborative voices of six diverse, accomplished, and dynamic professionals address the core challenges that hinder career growth—lack of direction, underdeveloped emotional intelligence, burnout, ineffective communication, and uncertainty in how to evolve as a leader.

Together, the authors have created far more than a book. *Career Breakthrough Playbook* is a movement—an invitation to step into your potential with courage, clarity, and action. Whether you're entering the workforce, navigating a career pivot, or aiming for executive leadership, this playbook delivers the structure and inspiration needed to move forward. A must-read for anyone serious about leveling up their professional journey. 5 Stars!!!"

— **Tiffany Wesley**,
FAADOM, RMTC, founder and
CEO of Elevation Dental Consulting,
integrator and senior advisor at Practice Booster

"*Career Breakthrough Playbook* is packed with insightful, actionable ideas for creating a professional life that's not just successful, but also sustainable, enjoyable, and deeply purposeful. It's the book I wish had been on my nightstand 30 years ago when I began my entrepreneurial journey! No matter where you are in your career—from intern to executive—this playbook will help you build a working life that evolves with you. It's more than a guide to professional success; it's an instruction manual for lifelong learning, growth, and fulfillment."

— **Lian Amber**,
CEO of BassBoss

"At a time when employment is increasingly transactional and short-lived, this book is a necessity. You may feel safe in your role right now, but what happens when your mentor retires, or your company is acquired? *Career Breakthrough Playbook* assembles perspectives on how to take charge of your own career, build resilience, and prepare for the unexpected."

— **Gaeron McClure**,
CPA, adjunct professor
of business ethics at the Fordham Gabelli School of Business,
author of *Selfish, Jealous, Shortsighted, Stubborn, and Ungrateful*

"If you haven't walked it, you can't impart it. *Career Breakthrough Playbook: Get Unstuck, Get Ahead* is a transformational masterpiece rooted in real-life experiences and professional insight. Divided into six sections, the book offers practical and relatable strategies to help professionals at any stage steer their careers forward. The principles are realistic, relevant, and grounded in lived experience, making them easy to connect with. This comprehensive guide emphasizes self-leadership, resilience, and continuous learning. It includes actionable steps, reflection questions, and tools for lasting career growth. Thank you for birthing this powerful and empowering resource."

— **Busola Afolayan**,
senior pastor at Glory Impact Christian Centre

"*Career Breakthrough Playbook* is a refreshingly practical and inspiring resource I'm excited to use in both coaching and leadership development. The career ownership tools and reflections provide a strong foundation for helping professionals take intentional control of their growth. Whether guiding others through transition or developing yourself, this book is a thoughtful, energizing guide I'll return to often in my coaching and consulting work."

— Jeni Yelton,
executive coach, OD consultant,
speaker, chief learning development officer
at Kairos Executive Programs

CAREER BREAKTHROUGH PLAYBOOK

GET UNSTUCK, GET AHEAD

MASTER THE SIX ESSENTIAL SKILLS THAT DRIVE PROFESSIONAL GROWTH AND SUCCESS

WILL LUKANG, HIBA TANVIR, DONYA SMIDA,
JOËL VUADENS-CHAN, NEHA DESHPANDE, ERIC E. EBRON

CONTENTS

PREFACE

Reflecting on my career journey, I realize how the standard advice given in high school often falls short of truly preparing us for the realities of the professional world. The roadmap seems simple: excel in school, get into a good college, graduate, and secure a job. The process appears straightforward: craft a resume, write a cover letter, apply for jobs, and ace the interview. Is it really that easy?

Landing your first job feels like a significant milestone, but there is rarely guidance on what comes next. My father once told me, "Do a good job, and your manager will promote you." I followed this advice for the first two years of my career—delivering results and hoping for recognition. Eventually, I was promoted to a team lead role, but I quickly realized that I had no training or preparation for leadership. Like many others, I had to learn how to manage people on the job, navigating real-world challenges without a clear roadmap. For valuable insights on leadership, I highly recommend reading my book, *Seeds of Leadership*.

A few years into my career, I transitioned to consulting roles, first in Singapore and later in the U.S. My career path unfolded more through a series of opportunities than through a deliberate plan. While I aspired to become a chief information officer or head of IT, I lacked a clear strategy for bridging the gap between where I was and where I wanted to be.

By my tenth year, I realized I needed a more intentional approach. I created a five-year plan with specific goals and began tracking my progress. For the first time, I had direction—and with it, a sense of control over my career. Each time I adjusted my strategy, I gained confidence and saw my aspirations take shape.

In February 2024, I attended a session with Steve Ericksen at Eventraptor about creating virtual events. One idea hit home: helping others overcome career stagnation.

If I'd had access to a career guide earlier in my journey, I could have been more intentional, confident, and further along. Inspired, I enrolled in Steve's program and took on the challenge of organizing my first virtual event. Although I had little experience, Steve and his team provided invaluable guidance, enabling me to navigate this new endeavor successfully.

As I planned the event, I reflected on my career journey and the lessons I learned along the way. A question arose: What if I could turn my experiences into something meaningful for others by providing the guidance I had often wished for?

This book grew from that very aspiration.

How This Book Came to Be?

The co-authors of this book are all past guests on the *IWillAim Podcast*. Through our conversations, I saw that their diverse expertise could offer invaluable insights to anyone seeking a thoughtful, strategic career plan. Each co-author brings to this project their unique knowledge and lived experience, sharing practical advice to help you navigate your professional journey. Together, we've created a comprehensive guide to equip you with the tools and strategies you need for success.

Who This Book Is For?

This book is for professionals at various stages of their careers, whether you're just starting out, stepping into a team lead role, or taking charge of your growth as a mid-level manager. If you're ready to take ownership of your career with clarity and purpose, this book is for you.

What Areas of Career Growth Does This Book Cover?

This guide is divided into six key sections, each focused on helping you level up, lead effectively, and thrive in your career:

1. **Career Guidance**: practical advice to help you confidently chart your path.

2. **Emotional Intelligence Mastery for Rising Professionals**: tools for managing yourself and your professional relationships effectively.

3. **Stress Management 101 for High Achievers**: techniques for navigating workplace pressures while advancing professionally.

4. **The Art of Effective Networking**: proven methods for building meaningful connections and expanding your influence.

5. **Public Speaking for Success**: guidance on expressing your ideas with impact and clarity.

6. **Leadership Blueprint: Becoming Unstuck and Unstoppable**: a roadmap for becoming a leader who inspires and empowers others.

My Vision for This Book

My goal is to provide you with a practical guide that helps you navigate the complexities of your career with confidence and purpose. Whether you're looking to build momentum or break free from stagnation, this book offers the insights and tools you need to take charge of your professional journey.

Here's to your success: may you move forward with intention, growth, and the confidence to thrive.

Will Lukang

SECTION 1

CAREER GUIDANCE
By Will Lukang

CHAPTER 1
The Making of Will

Growing up, my parents owned a convenience store, and I began helping out when I was just five years old. I noticed they employed four people, and as I got older, I learned they paid those employees a biweekly salary. That early exposure gave me my first glimpse into the difference between owning a small business and working for someone else. I continued working for my parents through college, and after graduating, I managed our family business for two years. The hands-on experience I gained during this time played a crucial role in shaping my career.

Throughout my education, my parents consistently emphasized the importance of good grades as the key to better job prospects. They encouraged us to excel in school and made it clear that a college degree was essential for unlocking the best opportunities.

Learning About Business

When I was 13 and a freshman in high school, I helped my father with the year-end inventory for our family business. He explained that knowing our closing inventory from the previous year was essential for establishing a starting point for the new year. That experience deepened my understanding of the diligence required to run a business and showed me how vital it is to keep accurate books and records.

Working for my parents taught me an early lesson: there are two fundamental ways to earn a living as an adult, either by owning a business or working for someone else. I knew I'd likely follow the second path since I didn't have the money to start my own business. However, I often wondered what it would be like to be my own boss. As a kid, the idea of being "the boss" sounded exciting, but I did not know how much work actually goes into owning a business.

Discovering My Passion for Software Development

In my senior year of high school, a small group of students were offered the chance to take a software programming class. To qualify, we had to maintain a certain GPA and pass an assessment exam. I'd already been introduced to programming by my older brother, who was four years ahead of me, so I applied, took the exam, and qualified. Programming quickly became my favorite subject. Still, at the time, I had no idea that computer science was an actual college major.

My parents insisted I study commerce and major in management, convinced I wasn't as academically strong as my siblings. Reluctantly, I took the entrance examination for the University of Santo Tomas (UST) College of Commerce. Back then, students didn't have to declare their major until the end of their sophomore year. I knew I didn't want to pursue management—I was hoping to qualify for Economics or earn a good enough grade to pass the accounting entrance exam.

I passed the entrance examination and enrolled in the UST College of Commerce. As my sophomore year ended, I applied for admission to major in economics and also took the accounting admission test. I was accepted into the economics program. A few days later, I learned I had passed the test and had been enrolled as an accounting major.

While in college, I took some programming courses. I enrolled in a couple of classes, and because I excelled in them, I felt validated in my desire to become a software engineer.

During my senior year, I participated in a computer quiz contest at the College of Commerce and placed third. The top three contestants were chosen to represent our college in the intercollegiate competition. Historically, our college had never made it past the preliminary rounds, but that year was different. After the eliminations, we ranked in the top three and advanced to the semifinals. We placed second, reaching the finals for the first time. It was uncharted territory, but we were confident in our skills and knowledge.

In the final round, the competition came down to the last question. We answered correctly, winning the first intercollegiate quiz competition for our college. Later, we represented our school at the national level and ranked in the top 15 out of over 50 schools.

Facing Family Expectations

After graduating, I attended a review class for several months to prepare for the Certified Public Accountant (CPA) board exam, one of the most challenging in the Philippines, with a pass rate of less than 20%. I struggled during the review and often questioned my ability to perform well. Still, I gave it everything I had. In the last three weeks of preparation, I studied late into the night, determined to consolidate my knowledge and strengthen the areas where I felt weakest.

The board examination is held over two weekends, with four subjects tested each Saturday and Sunday. After completing the final exam, I went to bed relieved and hopeful. But at 2:30 a.m. the following morning, my father woke me up and told me it was time for me to manage our family store. It had been my parents' plan all along, driven by their belief that I wasn't as capable as my siblings. I was devastated. I had an offer from SGV & Co. (an EY professional firm), one of the top accounting firms in the Philippines, and I had worked so hard with that future in mind. I couldn't hold back my tears; it felt like all my effort had led me not to the career I dreamed of, but to a path I hadn't chosen.

Despite my disappointment, I honored my parents' wishes and reluctantly took over the store. Some may wonder why I didn't push back, but in my culture, it is uncommon—if not unthinkable—for children to defy their parents' decisions.

When you are not passionate about what you do, getting up every day for work can feel like a battle. Nevertheless, I remained disciplined. I wanted my parents to see that I was mature enough to handle responsibility, even though I was unhappy. Many days felt like a waste of time, but I still put forth my best effort. The workdays were long, with no weekends or holidays off, and it became harder and harder to motivate myself to care about the work.

Whenever I met up with friends, I felt a pang of embarrassment. I had nothing new to share except the same update: I was working at my parents' store. My friends spoke excitedly about their training, the new skills they were learning, and the promotions they'd received. Eventually, I stopped attending our gatherings. It felt like I was falling further and further behind.

There was one aspect of my job that I thoroughly enjoyed, though: interacting with customers and making sure they felt seen and cared for. My father knew I was unhappy. At one point, he offered a compromise and suggested I attend law school while continuing to work at the store. I seriously considered it and even studied for the LSAT exam. But deep down, I knew I wouldn't be happy as a lawyer. What I truly wanted was to become a software engineer. Eventually, I told my father I wasn't going to pursue a law degree.

An Unexpected Success

The day the board exam results were released was always a mix of excitement and anxiety. I felt nervous but eager to check for my friends' names, even though I had no intention of looking up my own. I didn't believe I had passed.

I arrived at the store at 3:30 a.m., and about an hour later, I asked someone to buy a newspaper. When it arrived, I quickly scanned the summary: only 18% of test-takers had passed. My heart sank. With over 10,000 people taking the exam, that meant thousands had failed.

I began searching for my friends' names but couldn't find any of them. Suddenly, our phone rang, startling me. The caller congratulated me, saying they had seen my name in the newspaper. Stunned at first, I was soon overwhelmed with joy. I kept scanning the list, hoping to find my friends' names, but none of the six was there.

I called one of them. He congratulated me, but our conversation was brief. In that moment, I realized that sometimes you can't fully celebrate your success when those around you are struggling.

For the first time, my parents were proud of my accomplishment, and I finally experienced what it felt like to bring them genuine joy. My father even hosted a small celebration at the volunteer firehouse. For years, I had watched my siblings earn academic honors while I stood quietly in the background. Their achievements were always met with praise, while I was reminded of what I lacked. But despite that, I had always been proud of them. And now, at last, I had something of my own to celebrate with them—something I could be proud of, too.

Choosing My Path

After working for my parents for a year, I felt unfulfilled. I did not enjoy my job and, deep down, I couldn't see myself doing it long term. As my second year ended, I decided it was time to tell my parents that I wanted to pursue a career as a software engineer.

One day, I found the courage to tell my mother that I no longer wanted to work at the convenience store. I wanted to build a career developing applications and solving real-world problems as a software engineer. She was initially disappointed, but fortunately, my sister announced she would take over the business after graduating from college. That gave me the freedom to finally follow my passion.

It's important to remember that even when you choose a path, it doesn't have to be permanent. You can pivot. You can change jobs. You can start a new business. Don't get stuck chasing perfection. Sometimes, walking through one door, even if it's not the right one, gives you clarity about which direction you're truly meant to go.

CHAPTER 2
Find Your Path

Early on, I recognized that life offers at least two paths at the conclusion of one's academic journey: starting a business or working for someone else. While working with my father, I enjoyed running my own business, but I encountered two significant challenges.

First, I was unsure about what type of business I wanted to begin. I knew I didn't want to compete with my parents' business. Second, and more importantly, I lacked the capital to start a venture. Some might suggest taking out a loan, but at 20 years old, the idea of incurring debt was daunting without a solid business concept.

Here are some of the key points I considered:

Choice	Start your own business	Work for someone else
Capital	Upfront capital required	No capital needed
Decision making	You make the decisions	You follow others' decisions early in your career, gaining influence only later
Income generating power	Unlimited income and opportunities that come with significant risk	Income potential limited by fixed salary
Control	You are in control	No control because you work for someone else (but you can change jobs)

Freedom	Greater freedom	Limited, based on your assignment and position
Trajectory	Unlimited up and down	Limited based on how good your manager is in helping you grow
International Exposure	Limited because our business was a brick-and-mortar store in a marketplace	As a software engineer, there are opportunities to be an overseas contract worker

Based on the analysis above, I decided to pursue a career working for someone else.

If, like me, you realize that starting your own business isn't the right path, that decision can be a powerful turning point. The next step is to identify the skills you can bring to a potential employer. For example, are you adept at problem-solving, writing, teaching, or hands-on work? Be ready to showcase your strengths.

I recommend you take a structured evaluation to assess your abilities and identify your strengths, weaknesses, and growth opportunities. The evaluation section in this chapter will help you get a clear picture of where you are now, where you want to be, and the gap in between. That clarity is key to making informed, intentional career decisions.

If you're an experienced professional, you may choose to skip the remaining of this chapter, as it focuses on identifying your strengths and preparing to land a job. Before you move on, though, I'd like to share a personal story.

Despite enjoying years of consistent success as an executive, I unexpectedly lost my job because of a merger and acquisition. After dedicating 17 years of my life to one company, I suddenly found myself unemployed.

Fortunately, I had taken ownership of my career. I made it a habit to update my resume at least once a year to keep it current. I stayed active on

LinkedIn, engaged with my network, and responded to requests for help. I also prioritized continuous learning to remain relevant and adaptable in a constantly changing landscape.

The truth is, most of us will experience a career disruption at some point. The key is to be prepared, because it's always better to be ready than caught off guard. Ultimately, I chose to pivot. I pursued entrepreneurship and co-founded a company called Kairos Executive Programs. After working for others for 33 and a half years, I discovered it's never too late to pursue your dream.

Career Path Evaluation

Section 1: Strengths Assessment

By completing this section, you will identify your most marketable skills and gain insight into how you handle challenges, feedback, and pressure. This reflection will provide you with a clearer picture of your professional strengths.

1. What are the top three skills at which you excel?

2. What unique talents or abilities set you apart from others in your industry?

3. What are you naturally good at? (Your core strengths)

4. When facing challenges, what personal qualities help you overcome them?

5. What positive feedback do you frequently receive from colleagues, clients, or mentors?

6. In which areas do you feel most confident when making decisions or taking action?

7. What accomplishments make you proud? What strengths contributed to those successes?

8. How do you typically perform under pressure? What strengths help you stay effective?

9. How do you contribute to a team's success?

Section 2: Improvement Areas

This section is designed to help you take a step back and assess areas for improvement. By identifying recurring challenges, you can transform them into learning opportunities. Additionally, it encourages you to reflect on skill gaps that may hold you back from reaching your full potential.

1. What professional or personal skills do you believe need improvement?

2. What recurring challenges or obstacles do you encounter in your career or personal development?

3. Have you received any constructive feedback regarding areas where you struggle? If so, what was that feedback?

4. What situations make you feel uncertain or uncomfortable?

5. Do you have any habits that negatively affect your productivity or relationships?

6. In which areas do you tend to procrastinate or avoid taking action?

7. Are there any skill gaps that are preventing you from achieving your next level of success?

8. How do you handle criticism, and does it impact your confidence?

Section 3: Opportunities for Growth

This section encourages you to analyze trends in your field. The saying, "What got you here won't get you to the next level," emphasizes the need for continuous upskilling and stepping outside your comfort zone to stay ahead. Facing your fears is essential for growth, and every small step toward self-improvement is a step in the right direction.

1. What trends or changes in your industry could create new opportunities for you?

2. Can you develop skills that will make you more competitive in your field?

3. What relationships (mentors, networks, partnerships) could help you grow?

4. Could you enhance your work by leveraging new technologies, tools, or resources?

5. How can you expand your visibility, influence, or credibility within the industry?

6. Are there personal or professional development opportunities (such as courses, certifications, or coaching) that could help you improve?

7. Are there projects, roles, or experiences you should pursue to challenge yourself?

8. What fears or limiting beliefs might prevent you from seizing new opportunities?

Create an Action Plan

After completing your assessments, create a structured plan to improve yourself and take action. Use the SMART criteria to guide your planning:

S - Specific: Define clear and actionable goals. For example, enroll in an artificial intelligence course to enhance your knowledge. Specify the institution you will attend.

M - Measurable: Ensure that your progress can be tracked. For instance, aim to complete the AI course by the end of Q2 with a passing grade or strive for an A.

A - Actionable: Your goals must be something you can actively work towards. Make sure they are well-defined and not vague.

R - Realistic: Your goals should be achievable based on your time, resources, and commitments.

T - Time-bound: Set a deadline. For example, plan to complete the certification within one year.

Next, identify the types of jobs you are interested in, so you can prepare to apply for those positions. If you plan to become an entrepreneur, outline when, what, and how you will launch your business.

Accountability and Progress Tracking

I highly recommend finding an accountability partner—someone who shares similar personal or professional goals. Together, you can share your plans and hold bi-monthly check-ins to stay on track.

Having an accountability partner benefits you in two main ways: *Motivation and Commitment.* Knowing that someone will check in on your progress significantly increases your likelihood of staying committed to your goals.

Friendly Competition. You can gamify your progress by comparing how well you meet your goals against your accountability partner.

I have used this approach many times throughout my career, and it has consistently kept me on track because I knew I had to report my progress. While setbacks may occur, the key is to understand why they happened, take responsibility, and adjust your plan accordingly.

Remember, this is your plan and your future. The time and effort you invest in self-improvement today will shape your success tomorrow. Stay disciplined, stay committed, and most importantly, believe in your ability to achieve your goals.

Your Professional Story: Resume & LinkedIn Done Right

Once you have identified your strengths and what you excel at, it's time to prepare your resume and LinkedIn profile and begin your job search.

What is a resume? It is a formal document that summarizes your professional experience, education, skills, and achievements. A well-crafted resume highlights your qualifications and makes a strong case for why an employer should consider you for a role or arrange an interview.

Here are the key elements of a resume:

1. *Header.* Include your name, contact information (email address and physical address), and job title (if applicable).

2. *Summary or Objective.* Write a brief statement that highlights your career goals or notable professional achievements.

3. *Work Experience.* List your internships and job experiences in chronological order. Be sure to include your accomplishments and emphasize how you added value in each role. Whenever possible, use percentages to quantify your achievements.

4. *Education.* Detail your educational background, including degrees, certifications, and relevant coursework.

5. *Skills*. Highlight your technical skills, soft skills, and any industry-specific abilities.

6. *Projects*. Showcase significant projects, including a portfolio or repository of your work.

7. *Volunteer Work* (optional). Demonstrate your community involvement and any additional skills gained through volunteer experiences.

A resume is typically 1-2 pages long and should be customized for the specific role you are applying for. While I'm not a resume expert, it's a good idea to create a resume and seek feedback from your professor, advisor, or friends' parents. A resume is essential for representing you during a job application.

Sample Resume

Will Lukang, (Certification, Credential, etc)
111.111.1111 | youremail@domain.com | location | linkedin.com/in/first-lastname

PROFESSIONAL SUMMARY

Showcase your accomplishments. Include specific benefits or improvements.
Use bullet points; do not use objective statements.
Study body or club leadership position.
Contest or research accomplishments.

Expertise/Skills

Problem-Solving - Bookkeeping - Team Collaboration - Communication
Presentation - Client Management - Design Thinking

EXPERIENCE

JOB TITLE

Date - from - present

Location, State

Use this paragraph to summarize your role and highlight your accomplishments. Include details on promotion or taking on more responsibilities. List each of your accomplishments using action verbs such as "delivered," "collaborated," or "led." Be specific and include the impact you made.

For example:

- *Increased sales by 10% year over year.*

- *Improved operational efficiency by 5% by implementing a new automated workflow.*

EDUCATION & CERTIFICATION

Bachelor of Science in Accounting /University Name, City, State

Year

You can include roles in your school, awards, and certifications.

Cover Letter

There are occasions when you're required to submit a cover letter alongside your resume when you're applying for a job. A cover letter is a formal document that introduces you to the employer, expresses your interest in the position, and explains why you are a strong candidate. A well-crafted cover letter complements your resume by providing context for your experience and showcasing your enthusiasm for the role.

Use the cover letter to:

- *Introduce yourself:* Briefly explain who you are and why you are interested in the job.

- *Highlight relevant skills and experience:* Emphasize which of the skills and experiences align with the job description.

- *Demonstrate interest and enthusiasm*: Show your excitement about the role and mention specific things you admire about the company.

- *Request an interview:* End with a call to action, requesting an interview or further discussion.

Your cover letter should be structured as follows:

- *Header*: Include your contact information and employee details.

- *Salutation*: Use a formal greeting addressed to the hiring manager.

- *Introduction*: Start with a strong opening statement that expresses your interest in the position.

- *Body Paragraph(s)*: Discuss your relevant work experience, key skills, and how you can contribute to the company.

- *Conclusion*: Thank the employer, reiterate your interest, and express your desire to move forward.

- *Signature*: End with a formal closing (e.g., "Sincerely") and your full name.

A customized cover letter should be created for each job. It should be concise and professional.

LinkedIn

For the next step, I suggest creating a LinkedIn profile. LinkedIn (www.linkedin.com) is a site widely used for networking and job hunting. You can start by browsing my profile: https://www.linkedin.com/in/lukangwill/.

I used a LinkedIn expert to help me craft my profile. Start by entering all your information. Once completed, send it to your advisor for review and request feedback.

What is LinkedIn?

LinkedIn is a professional networking platform for career development, business connections, and industry discussions. Users can create profiles showcasing their experience, skills, achievements, and certifications and join professional groups.

Whether you own your business or work for someone else, create a LinkedIn profile. You can use it to manage your brand or showcase your company's services or offerings. I've used LinkedIn for years and connected/collaborated with many people. I can vouch for its importance to your career.

You can use LinkedIn to search for a job or connect with recruiters.

Nailing Your Interview: Tips for Success

By applying everything you've learned so far, you're well on your way to landing your first job interview. Making a strong first impression is a great start, but in order to succeed, you'll need to prepare thoroughly for the interview itself. This includes researching the company, practicing your responses to common questions, and being ready to showcase your skills and enthusiasm.

As you prepare, think also of how you will present yourself. Start by reflecting on the following questions:

- What is your story?

- What are your skills?

- How will you add value to the company?

- What projects or part-time work did you do that relate to the job?

- What accomplishments do you have that will be relevant to the role?

It is essential to know the company you're applying to. Research the following:

- What are their mission and vision?

- What is their business all about?

- What sets them apart from others in the industry?

When preparing for the interview, rehearse with a friend or mentor. Practice interviews will help you feel more confident and refine your responses. Preparation is key to your success, so focus on being authentic and staying true to who you are.

On the Day of the Interview

The big day has arrived. To set yourself up for success:

- Get to bed early the night before so you're well rested.

- Arrive on time or, even better, arrive a little early to give yourself some buffer time.

- Dress for the occasion—your attire should align with the company's culture and the position.

- Be authentic; don't fabricate stories or answers. If you don't know something, be honest. Let the interviewer know you don't know the answer, but you will research it and follow up with them.

- Always have questions prepared for the interviewer.

- Before you leave, confirm that you've answered all their questions and thank them for their time.

- After the interview, follow up with a thank you note, either handwritten or via email. I personally prefer sending a handwritten note, as it is more memorable and personal.

Key Takeaways:

- **Assess your overall abilities:** Take a moment to evaluate your strengths and areas for growth.

- **Choose your path:** Identify the direction you want to take, based on your skills and passions.

- **Know your gifts:** Find something you're truly good at and understand your unique strengths.

- **Take job applications seriously:** Treat each application with care. Research the company thoroughly to understand their mission, vision, and what's currently happening with them. Be ready to explain why you want to work for them.

- **Prepare for the interview:** Do your homework, practice your responses, and be ready to demonstrate your skills and enthusiasm.

- **Be yourself and present for the interview:** Authenticity is key. Stay present and true to who you are. Ask questions and show interest.

CHAPTER 3

Own Your Career

Reflecting on my journey, I often wished I had a guide to help me navigate my career. I frequently felt lost and confused, struggling to move from point A to point B. Career growth isn't always straightforward, but having a mentor allows you to create a solid plan and provides the right tools to navigate challenges.

Without guidance, I felt stuck, and relying on chance in my career was daunting. I worked hard, yet I still missed out on promotions, often without any clear reason. Have you ever experienced something similar? At some point in our careers, we all encounter setbacks like these. That sense of helplessness and undervaluation can be mitigated if we plan, communicate our goals, and work strategically toward achieving them.

Is It Your Manager's Job to Guide You?

Some may argue that a manager's role is to support and guide their employees. While this is true, many managers are not trained to lead effectively. They often feel overwhelmed by their responsibilities, juggling their tasks while ensuring their teams meet deadlines. Many managers learn through trial and error rather than through structured leadership training.

I remember my first job when I was promoted to team lead. I was excited at first, but that excitement quickly turned into worry. How was I supposed to manage people who had been my peers just a day before? I learned the hard way that some relationships changed. In some cases, this change was due to people trying to use our friendship as an excuse for not doing their jobs, while in others, it stemmed from jealousy.

Like most people, I had assumed that my manager would look out for my career. While some managers genuinely care about their employees' growth, many are primarily focused on getting the work done. It's important to recognize which type of manager you have so that you can plan accordingly. When you take ownership of your career, you don't have to worry about your manager's priorities because you'll be proactive in setting goals and having meaningful discussions about your professional development.

Take Control of Your Career

What if I told you that you have the power to take control of your career? By reading this book, you are already taking the first step toward owning your professional journey.

Real progress begins when you take charge. This book has been written by a team of co-authors with one mission: to equip you with the tools, insights, and confidence you need to move forward in your career with clarity, confidence, and purpose.

The Reality of Workplace Dissatisfaction

Let's look at the data:

- 79% of employees leave their jobs due to a lack of appreciation from their employer (Happier.com).

- Only 51% of employees are satisfied with their jobs—meaning nearly half of workers are unhappy (Pew Research, 2023).

- 43% of employees feel stuck in their careers—uncertain how to move forward (Pew Research, 2023).

- Nearly 50% of workers are considering leaving their jobs in 2024—a number even higher than during the Great Resignation (CNBC, May 2024).

As a manager, you have the power to make a significant difference in your employees' lives. If you're an employee, consider this your wake-up call: it's time to take ownership of your career. Managers can have a profound impact on their team members. It's essential to take a genuine interest in their aspirations and actively support their growth. This means helping them gain the skills and experiences that will move them closer to their goals. Throughout my career, I've prioritized understanding each team member's goals and actively supporting them in achieving those aspirations.

Aligning individual desires with the company's objectives can be challenging because they don't always match up perfectly. However, when you invest the time to bridge that gap, you often uncover opportunities that serve both the employee and the organization. I emphasize this because I have successfully navigated this process many times and have seen how it positively influences job satisfaction and morale among employees.

A Personal Story

Early in my career, I was tasked with leading the rewrite of a critical application. As the team lead, I was assigned a group of eight people, all older than me. Many of them were in their 30s, 40s, and 50s.

I could see the doubt in their eyes. How could this young guy possibly lead us? For weeks, they challenged my ideas. I knew I had to prove myself and earn their trust. So, I focused on showing up consistently: demonstrating my knowledge, supporting the team, and making sure we stayed ahead of schedule. Eventually, they accepted me as their leader, and together we delivered the project six weeks early.

During my one-on-one meetings with my manager, I expressed my interest in being promoted. He told me I was a top performer and assured me he supported my request. I followed up multiple times throughout the year, continuing to deliver results.

Then came the promotion list. My name wasn't on it. I was shocked. I scheduled a meeting with my manager. When I asked him why I'd been passed over, he had no explanation. He looked at me, speechless. Have you been in this situation? You work hard. You exceed expectations. Even so, you get passed over.

That experience was a turning point for me. I realized I had been so focused on getting the work done that I missed the sign on the wall: my manager wasn't invested in my growth. His priority was simply meeting deadlines, not developing people.

I felt anger, frustration, and disappointment, but I took action instead of dwelling on it. From that moment on, I decided to take ownership of my career, plan my development, and track my progress. Eventually, I left that company for a better opportunity.

If you're a manager, take care of your employees. If you don't, they will leave, and you'll face the costs of hiring, training, and lost productivity.

The worst experience for an employee is feeling betrayed. If someone isn't ready to level up, have that conversation. But not telling people where they stand? That's unacceptable.

I take full ownership of how I responded to that experience. And from that day forward, I committed to taking action and seeking the support and guidance I needed to grow.

A Common Career Journey

Over the past twenty years, I've observed a recurring pattern: people working tirelessly, sacrificing weekends, late nights, and family time, in pursuit of promotions and better pay. Some even cancel vacations when asked to help. They see others climbing the corporate ladder and feel pressured to do the same, even if they are unsure how to proceed.

Meanwhile, they are often managed by overwhelmed and untrained supervisors who are just trying to keep things running smoothly. Many hope their manager will advocate for them, but too often, managers are focused solely on hitting their own targets. As a result, employees wait and work even harder, hoping someone will notice their efforts. Yet, promotions continue to elude them.

Does this sound familiar? You're ambitious, diligent, and hungry for growth, yet it feels like an invisible chain keeps you trapped in an endless cycle of frustration and stagnation. After being passed over for promotions multiple times, you may start to question if all the effort is even worth it.

But what if I told you it doesn't have to be this way?

You can choose today to take ownership of your career. By reading this book, applying its insights, and taking proactive steps, you can build a career where *you* are in the driver's seat.

Key Takeaways:

- Don't leave your career to chance.

- Be in the driver's seat and steer your career.

- If you want an opportunity or promotion, share that with your manager. They are not mind readers. Articulate it, but don't repeat it often.

- Establish a good relationship with your manager, because they can help you achieve your goals.

CHAPTER 4
Ten Tips for Managing Your Career

With over three decades of experience leading and developing people, I have compiled a list of career tips that I have personally applied and tested throughout my journey. I implemented many of these strategies with my colleagues and witnessed measurable improvements in employee satisfaction and promotion outcomes. Looking back, I often wish I had a guide to follow in my early career. That's why I've written this book—to share my experiences and offer you a roadmap as you navigate your own career path.

Tip #1: Own Your Career

When I was passed over for a promotion, I felt frustrated and confused. The feedback I received was vague and generic, and it felt more like an excuse than a proper explanation. That experience pushed me to take full ownership of my career. Although this approach didn't eliminate every challenge, it led to more meaningful conversations with my managers and allowed me to outline my career path more clearly.

Don't rely on your manager to champion your cause or manage your career for you. The truth is that many managers simply aren't trained or prepared to help their employees grow. Depending solely on them can be a gamble and not yield a positive outcome.

Growing up, my dad told me to do my best work, and my manager would take care of me. While that advice holds some truth—because yes, some managers do care—most are too busy juggling their own responsibilities. I don't blame my parents for that perspective. But I've learned that if I want to steer my career in the right direction, I must take the wheel.

Sure, some managers will invest time in guiding you, but many are overwhelmed and not equipped to foster their employees' development. Many were promoted because they excelled as individual contributors and were never taught how to lead others effectively. Too often, "on-the-job training" becomes a catch-all excuse for the lack of proper guidance. If companies invested more time and resources in training their managers, the ripple effect could be significant, a more engaged and committed workforce.

In my situation, my manager was so busy that they had rarely had time for mentorship or discussing my career aspirations. That's when I realized something crucial: I needed to stop waiting and start acting. I had to take control of my growth.

I encourage you to do the same. Start today. There's a saying: *The best time to plant a tree was yesterday. The next best time is now.* The sooner you identify what you want and commit to pursuing it, the sooner you'll build the career you deserve.

Key Takeaways:

- Owning your career gives you the power to define your path from point A to B. It doesn't guarantee everything will go exactly as planned, but it allows you to have informed, intentional conversations about your future and gives you the perspective to understand what you need to work on to reach your goals.

- Taking ownership is an active, strategic approach to building a fulfilling career.

Tip #2: Know What's Required to Get Promoted

If you want to get promoted, you must understand what's required. It's not enough simply to want the title or the raise. You need clarity on the expectations for the next level and where you currently stand. Start by identifying the role you're aiming for. What does success in that position look like? What steps do you need to take to get there? Many professionals aspire to a promotion without fully grasping the criteria for advancement.

Take the time to review the employee handbook or your company's website. Familiarize yourself with the promotion guidelines and assess each requirement honestly. Have you met them all? If not, seek your manager's help to gain the necessary exposure or opportunities. Every organization has its own process, whether formal or informal, for how promotions are decided. Regardless of how clearly it's documented, one truth remains: there are always specific criteria behind every advancement.

Throughout my career, when someone tells me they're ready for a promotion, I often ask: "Do you know what's required for the next level?" More often than not, the answer is, "I'm not sure." If you don't know the criteria, how can you evaluate whether you qualify? Some people might say that they're doing great in their current job. And while that's important, performing well in your current role doesn't automatically show that you are ready for a promotion. Understanding the specific requirements can help you evaluate how close you are to meeting them.

In my last role, the promotion criteria encompassed five categories. A candidate had to meet expectations in all five to be considered. It is essential to guide individuals in discussing each criterion and having them justify how their actions meet those requirements. Reviewing each category will provide insights into your readiness for promotion. If you find you are missing one or two categories, these can serve as discussion points with your manager on how they can assist you in gaining the necessary exposure or opportunities. Together, you can develop a plan to meet those criteria. More importantly, when you discuss this with your manager, you'll gain their support because they will recognize your interest in advancing your career. This process of review and validation offers a clearer picture of your current standing.

Personally, I've had moments where I thought I was ready for a promotion only to realize I met just three out of five requirements. Sure, it was disappointing at first, but it gave me direction by making me aware of which areas I had to improve.

Wanting a promotion is one thing. But knowing what it takes and actively working toward it is what sets high performers apart.

If you're serious about owning your career, don't wait for someone else to spell it out.

While promotion criteria may vary from company to company, I have yet to encounter one that does not have at least a general outline of what it takes to be promoted. Investigate the requirements, start the conversation, and create a plan of action. Managers are far more likely to support your growth when they see your commitment and preparation. And when the time comes, they'll be equipped to advocate for your promotion with confidence.

Key Takeaways:

- Understanding the criteria for promotion is essential if you want to move up.

- The sooner you learn what's required, the sooner you can close the gaps and have meaningful, strategic conversations with your manager. It's not just about working harder; it's about working smarter and with intention.

Tip #3: Identify and Amplify Your Strengths

You might ask, "Why should I focus on my strengths? I'm already good at them."

That's exactly why.

Your strengths are your natural gifts, your talents, your superpowers. Maybe you're a whiz at math, an engaging communicator, or a standout presenter. These skills come naturally to you, but here's the catch: being good at something doesn't mean you've maxed out its potential.

There is always room to grow, even in the areas where you already shine. Take analytics, for example. If people regularly seek your help because you're great with numbers and data, you already bring value.

But what if you took it a step further? What if you explored how artificial intelligence could elevate your analytics skills? Or learned how to weave storytelling into your data presentations? Your new skill becomes a differentiator, something that sets you apart and significantly increases the value you bring to a business.

Not maximizing your strengths is a missed opportunity. Too often, people believe that being "good enough" is enough. But in today's fast-paced, competitive world, growth-minded professionals know great can always get greater.

As someone who coaches basketball and soccer, I've seen this firsthand. I've observed that top athletes always strive for improvement. The most talented athletes are rarely the ones who coast. They're the ones who put in extra reps, arrive early, and stay late. They're disciplined, energized, and focused not because they have to be, but because they're invested in becoming the best version of themselves. This dedication is an investment in their skills, not a sacrifice.

It's time to apply the same mindset to your career.

Exercise

1. **List three strengths.**

   Write down three things that come naturally to you. These are your signature skills.

2. **Identify ways to amplify them.**

   Could you take a class? Work with a mentor or coach? Apply your skills in a new, challenging context?

3. **Set a start date.**

   Put it on your calendar. If you don't schedule it, it won't happen.

4. **Set a deadline.**

   Create urgency by choosing a realistic date to achieve the first milestone.

5. **Take action.**

   Don't overthink it. Start today. Build momentum and celebrate small wins along the way.

Working on your strengths feels easier because it builds on what already brings you joy. That positive energy fuels motivation and makes the process of growth more rewarding.

Key Takeaways:

- Amplifying your strengths turns your natural talent into a superpower.

- Constant growth is energizing and fulfilling, and one of the fastest ways to create more value for yourself and your organization.

Tip #4: Turn Your Blind Spots into Strengths

Let's be honest: working on your blind spots isn't easy. It's uncomfortable, often frustrating, and, frankly, exhausting just to think about. But here's the truth: self-improvement isn't optional if you want to grow. It's a necessary step on the path to reaching your full potential.

That's why Tip #3 focused on building from a place of strength. Starting with what you're naturally good at helps you build momentum. That positive energy makes it easier to turn your attention to the more difficult areas, the blind spots that are your weaknesses.

Now, let's talk about these.

While you are enhancing your strengths, don't neglect your blind spots. Weaknesses, if left unaddressed, can make it difficult to reach the next level of your development. They often become the invisible ceiling that keeps you from reaching the next level.

Exercise

- **Identify two weaknesses.**

  Reflect honestly. What do you struggle with? Is it public speaking? Delegating? Time management?

- **Dig into the why.**

  Why do these areas challenge you? What patterns or habits contribute to the struggle?

- **Outline improvement actions.**

  What steps could you take to get better? Could you read a book, take a course, shadow a peer, or ask for feedback?

- **Create a plan.**

  Write it down. Be specific. Include small steps and support resources.

- **Assign a due date.**

  Put a timeline on your growth. Treat it like any other performance goal.

- **Take action.**

  Progress happens step by step. Start now. Chip away at it, one step at a time.

I often use my manager's feedback as a foundation for my improvement list. If you're unsure where to start, review your last performance evaluation. Even if you disagree with the feedback, it reflects how others perceive you, which matters. You can't address what you don't acknowledge. Use that input to create your improvement roadmap.

Key Takeaways:

- **Your weaknesses will limit your growth if you ignore them.**

  Facing them head-on may be uncomfortable, but doing so creates space for transformation. The sooner you take ownership, the sooner you unlock your full potential.

- **Not every weakness needs to become a strength.**

  If you're in a position to delegate tasks you're not great at, that's okay. Just make sure you own the outcome. Accountability is nonnegotiable.

Tip #5: Change Unproductive Behaviors

The next point is critical because it can derail careers, even for the most talented professionals. You must change unproductive behaviors. You may work hard turning your weaknesses into strengths, but if you continue holding onto unproductive habits, your progress will be limited.

Think of it this way: you can put in the effort to climb the ladder, but if you're shaking it as you go, you're only making it harder to reach the top.

For example, I'm working with a manager who rarely plans ahead. Everything becomes a last-minute scramble, always urgent and always stressful. As a result, the team often has to stay late to get things done. While the manager is aware of the issue, they haven't taken meaningful steps to address it. Over time, team members leave or transfer because they can't keep up with the constant chaos.

Another example of unproductive behavior is consistently showing up late.

It may seem like a small thing, but consistently being late to meetings damages your credibility. It sends a message that says, "My time matters more than yours." People notice. They remember. And over time, they stop trusting you.

Finally, interrupting others during conversations is another example of unproductive behavior. Even when it's unintentional, it can still come across as disruptive and disrespectful. It signals that you're not truly listening, which can shut down communication and hinder collaboration.

How to Identify Unproductive Behaviors

Sometimes, we're too close to our own habits to see what's not working. That's why asking for feedback is a game-changer. Try asking those around you these simple questions:

- Is there anything I do that affects your ability to work well with me?

- What's one thing I could stop doing to be more effective?

You might be surprised at what you hear, but it's a gift. Feedback helps you stop doing things that annoy, distract, or frustrate others, and start showing up as the kind of teammate or leader others want to work with. Feedback helps you grow.

Key Takeaways:

- Unproductive behaviors, no matter how small, can sabotage your career. Be honest with yourself.

- If you're not sure what needs to change, ask for feedback. Then, take that insight seriously and do the work to improve. Success isn't just about what you do well; it's also about what you're willing to stop doing.

Tip #6: Find a Mentor

I wish I had understood the power of mentoring earlier in my career. I first learned about mentoring four years into my journey, while consulting for KPMG. At the end of each project, my manager met with me to review what went well and what could be improved. It was refreshing to reflect on our work together.

At first, his interest in my professional development and the time he dedicated to our conversations, which included reflecting on lessons learned and celebrating our successes, surprised me. Why was he taking this time with me, when he didn't seem to do it with others? One day, I finally asked him. He smiled and said, "Because I'm mentoring you."

That moment changed how I viewed development. He believed in me—he saw potential, talent, and discipline—and he invested time to help me grow. That's the heart of mentorship: someone helping you see further, go farther, and grow faster than you might on your own.

I am grateful for the opportunity to learn from someone with years of experience in the same field. He has guided me and helped me see things from a different perspective.

Mentorship is a powerful tool for both personal and professional development. It provides guidance, support, and insights from experience.

Here are some reasons why mentorship is vital:

- *Knowledge transfer:* Mentors share insights, knowledge, and best practices. It's pure wisdom that could take years to learn on your own. Mentees gain perspective and make better decisions based on knowledge shared by their mentor.

- *Career advancement:* Mentors help individuals set career goals, identify growth opportunities, and expand their network. They can become your champions, recommending you for promotions or leadership roles.

- *Confidence building:* A mentor offers encouragement, constructive feedback, and support. Mentees develop confidence by learning from their mentor's wins and failures.

- *Accountability for growth:* Mentors help you stay on track, provide clarity, and offer course corrections. They open doors and help you stay focused on meaningful progress.

- *Understanding organizational culture:* A mentor can help you navigate the unwritten rules of your organization. This guidance reduces turnover and helps you integrate more effectively.

- *Giving back:* Mentors pass on their knowledge, creating a lasting impact on future generations. Mentees often become mentors, paying forward the support they received.

Mentoring is a powerful relationship that benefits both the mentee and the mentor. It creates a ripple effect within the organization, fostering growth and mutual support.

Recognizing the value and impact of mentoring, I have made it a priority to seek mentors from whom I can gain advice and assistance. In turn, I have dedicated my time to helping others who are seeking guidance. At one point in my career, I had over 50 mentees, and I take pride in this because sharing your time and being there for others requires significant effort.

How do you find a mentor? My mentors are individuals I respect and admire for their conduct and approach. They vary in age, with some older and others younger. The mentoring relationship is not solely about age; it's more about experience related to what you have and what you want to learn. When I identify someone who I believe would make a great mentor, I ask them to take on that role and explain how I would benefit from their guidance. Initially, I was concerned about being turned down, but I've learned that most often, the response is positive. If someone says no, that's okay. It might simply mean that it's not the right fit. It's important to find a mentor who is committed to spending time with you. A good mentor is someone who cares about you and challenges you. They'll offer guidance, but they'll also push you to grow.

My current mentor works at the same company as I do, while others are in different industries. We may not share the same job, but it is refreshing to learn from their experiences and apply that knowledge to my own environment.

Throughout my career, I have maintained relationships with multiple mentees for over 20 years, many of whom I now consider friends.

Mentors can serve as powerful advocates within your organization. They challenge you, hold you accountable, look out for your best interests, and help advocate for your promotion. However, mentees must do their part by taking the initiative to schedule meetings and always showing up prepared. They need to show that they value their mentor's time by following up on takeaways from their sessions. Likewise, mentors should respect their mentees' time, avoid last-minute cancellations, and show genuine interest in their journey.

What if the arrangement isn't working?

There is no need to prolong a relationship that isn't beneficial for either party. As a mentee, it is important to communicate this to your mentor and move on. The same applies to mentors; if a mentee appears disengaged and does not act on feedback, it is best to be honest and let them know that your time cannot be invested in someone who is not serious about the mentor-mentee relationship.

Key Takeaways:

- Determine what you need help with and find a mentor who knows that domain well.

  Don't be afraid to ask for help—most people are more than willing to guide someone who shows initiative.

- If you've gained experience, be the person who gives back. Find a mentee and help them grow and develop.

- If you take action, you'll benefit from learning and helping others on their journey.

Tip #7: Create a Growth Plan

A growth plan is your personal blueprint for self-improvement. It's a clear, intentional way to track the habits, skills, and goals you want to build to create a better version of yourself. I've been using a growth plan for over 15 years. There's no need for a fancy tool or a special journal. I use a simple Excel spreadsheet, and it works beautifully. The key isn't the method you choose; it's the act of documenting your progress.

Below is for illustration purposes:

Amplifying	Training	Date	Status
Public speaking	Attend Ving Giang Stage Academy	March 2024	Completed
Podcast	Podcast Bootcamp by Jonathan Jones	July 2024	Completed
Coaching	Valerie Burton AOAA	March 2024	Completed

Improvement	Training	Date	Status
Read	Tricycle Effect by Dane Deutsch	August 2024	Completed
Publish my second book	Seed of Leadership	December 2024	Completed
Positive Psychology	Learn Positive Psychology	In progress	Fall behind
Mindfulness	Accomplishing Daily Micro Habits	Ongoing	On track for over 27 months
Learn more about AI	Read Leap Beyond AI	In progress	
Above and beyond	What	Date	Status
Podcast	EOY 50 episode	December 2024	52 episodes Completed
Host a Virtual Event	Career Breakthrough	September 2024	Completed
Create a short film	Consequence of Tomorrow on YouTube	October 2024	Completed
Create a new firm	Kairos Executive Programs LLC	August 2024	Completed

I review this list monthly to track my progress. It's my way of holding myself accountable. This exercise allows me to see everything I have on my plate and decide whether anything needs to shift based on my current circumstances. Some goals may become irrelevant over time, and that's okay. A growth plan isn't meant to be rigid. It's a living document that adapts with you and helps clarify what you want to work on throughout the year.

Use the list you created of your strengths to populate the "amplify" section. Then take the weaknesses you've identified and set stretch goals for improvement. I also recommend adding the task of eliminating unproductive behaviors under the improvement section and mark them as ongoing because these take time and intention to overcome.

This exercise encourages accountability and reinforces the most important truth: you own your career. As my friend Sandy Cerami says, "Ownership and accountability for your journey's effort is a sign of personal and professional maturity and progress."

This plan is yours. You choose the goals. You set the timelines. You do the work.

Avoid setting a year-end deadline when creating your growth plan. First, it is unrealistic. Second, it doesn't show that you are serious about self-improvement. You are in the driver's seat of your career. Where do you want to go? I assume you want to move forward, not backward.

Strive to find a balance between improvement and amplification because I know that working on strengths can bring energy and joy, while addressing weaknesses requires significant time and effort. Balancing both aspects is essential. Please start your plan today, so you're well on your way to making the progress you desire.

Key Takeaways:

- A growth plan lets you see the overall picture for that year. It keeps you focused, allows you to track your progress, and gives you space to celebrate your wins. A plan, no matter how simple, is better than having no plan at all.

- Having a plan is better than having no plan because you can track your progress and celebrate your successes.

Tip #8: Take Action and Track Progress

Once you've created your growth plan, it's time to take action. Pick one or two areas from your list and start working on them. Add them to your calendar as dedicated time blocks. Progress doesn't come from planning alone; it comes from taking action. Remember, the first step is always the hardest. Even the best plan won't get you anywhere if it stays on paper.

The truth is, the first step is always the hardest. Whether it's starting a workout routine, changing your diet, or building new habits, Day One is often the toughest, but it's also the first step towards a better tomorrow. Keep in mind that you're doing this for yourself, and if you have a family, you're doing it for them too. Personally, I find motivation in everything I do because I know I'm striving for my two daughters and my wife.

Back when we worked in the office, I kept pictures of my daughters on my desk. On tough days, I would glance at those photos and remind myself, "This is why I push through." That moment of perspective would reignite my motivation.

You need to find your own version of that "why." I can't decide that for you. What I can say is that you can take action today. As Warren Buffett once said, "You're enjoying shade today because someone planted that tree 20 years ago." If you don't start today, 20 years from now, you may look back and wonder, "What happened to my career? Why am I not successful?" You might have a fantastic plan, but without action, it won't come to fruition.

Once you take the first step, stay consistent. Focus on the daily grind: day one, day two, day three. That's where habits are formed. If you need help staying motivated, find someone who inspires you. Whether it's a mentor, a friend, a coach, or your own internal drive, tap into it regularly.

A few weeks in, you'll begin to feel good about your progress. Now is the time to track your accomplishments. How many tasks have you completed? Celebrate your successes along the way.

Be honest with yourself. If you're not making progress, reflect on what's holding you back and adjust your plan. I review mine each year and frequently move deadlines or even drop tasks that no longer serve me. That's not failure; it's wisdom. Not everything will stick, and that's okay.

I've started many projects out of a desire to learn, but sometimes I lose interest halfway through and stop. Some things simply don't work out because I gain little from them, and that's okay. The key is to keep an overview of your plan, using a color code for tracking.

When I complete a task, I mark it blue; I love seeing more blue on my list. A task in progress is marked green, similar to a project plan, while an uncompleted task is marked red. The more red I have, the more I push myself to get ahead and not just aim for a plan filled with green or blue. That color-coding helps me stay visually accountable. The more blue I see, the more motivated I get. If I notice too much red, I know it's time to refocus or change direction.

Stay engaged with the plan. Keep a high-level view of where you're headed and what's moving. Progress, not perfection.

Key Takeaways:

- Tracking your progress allows you to see your progress.

- If you're not progressing well, you can reflect on what is holding you back and adjust accordingly.

- If you're making good progress, celebrate your success and the hard work you've put in.

Tip #9: Find an Accountability Partner

An accountability partner is someone you team up with to share your goals and plans and hold each other accountable. They support your progress, check in regularly, and help you stay motivated. In return, you do the same for them. It's a powerful way to stay on track, especially when life gets busy or motivation fades.

How Do You Find an Accountability Partner?

Look for someone you trust, respect, and believe will show up consistently. This could be a friend, coworker, mentor, or anyone aligned with your goals. Choose someone who's as committed to their own growth as you are to yours.

How Does It Work?

Most accountability partners meet every two weeks to discuss their plans and progress. During your check-ins, you share what you've accomplished, what you're struggling with, and what you plan to tackle next. If either of you is falling behind, the other can offer encouragement, challenge your thinking, and help brainstorm next steps. These conversations create momentum.

I first learned about the power of accountability partners in 2013 at a John Maxwell Team event. On day two, I connected with a few attendees, and we decided to become accountability partners. There were five of us: two from Canada, one from Australia, and me.

We committed to bimonthly Zoom calls to support each other.

In our first session, we each set a goal. Mine was to run two Mastermind groups based on *The 21 Irrefutable Laws of Leadership.* Sharing that goal out loud added real weight. Knowing I had to report back pushed me to follow through. My partners gave me feedback, ideas, and encouragement. We all did the same for each other.

Over the next six months, we consistently met and made progress. By the end of that period, we had each achieved the goals we set. Eventually, as we became busier building our businesses, we phased out our meetings, but the impact stayed with me.

Key Takeaways:

- **It is hard to do things alone**.

- An accountability partner provides gentle pressure, motivation, and perspective.

- **When you're stuck, talk it through with someone who understands your journey**.

- You'll gain the clarity you need to move forward.

- **Find someone to walk with**.

- If you want to move faster and farther, don't walk alone.

Tip #10: Be Curious

Being curious shows a desire to learn, explore, and understand the world around us. It involves asking questions, seeking new experiences, trying new opportunities, and being open to different ideas. Curiosity drives both personal and professional growth, pushing us to broaden our horizons. It acts as a catalyst for innovation, learning, and enriching life experiences.

Demonstrating curiosity shows that you do not simply follow instructions and meet expectations. By asking questions and exploring solutions, you start to think beyond current challenges and responsibilities. Curiosity signals potential for growth, and leaders often seek innovative individuals who explore various options to address the challenges they face.

Some employees expect promotions because they complete their tasks and follow instructions. However, leaders typically look for curious, proactive individuals who can solve problems, collaborate effectively, and adapt to changing situations. While doing your job might get you noticed, it is not a guarantee of advancement.

Additionally, it is crucial for you to show genuine concern for your work and demonstrate that you prioritize your clients' best interests.

When your manager gives you feedback, follow through and own the process. Remember, focusing on personal development will increase your value in the workplace.

How do you improve your curiosity?

- *Ask qu*estions. Not just to check a box, but to really understand. Ask "why" and "how" to dig deeper. Seek out the reason behind a process or goal—not just what needs to be done, but why it matters.

- *Seek feedback and act on it.* Asking for feedback shows you're open to growth. Acting on it proves you're serious about getting better. It also shows your manager that you're invested in your own success.

- *Take on new experiences.* Step out of your comfort zone. Volunteer for new responsibilities or explore different roles. This expands your perspective and shows your adaptability. More importantly, your manager will notice that you're versatile and adaptable.

- *Connect with others.* Talk to people in similar or different roles. Learn what they do and see what you can apply to your own work. I call this *borrowed innovation.* Often, the best ideas come from outside your usual circle.

Key Takeaways:

- **Curiosity can be developed.**

  It might not feel natural at first, but with practice and intention, you can strengthen it.

- **Be curious.**

  If you want to level up, you need to stand out. The best way to do this is to be curious and apply the insights provided in this chapter.

Sometimes, even with a solid plan and consistent action, things don't unfold the way you expected. That doesn't mean you've failed. It simply means that you might be in the wrong environment. What matters most is that you showed up. You made the effort. You took ownership of your growth rather than leaving your career to chance. And when the results didn't align with your goals, you had the courage to reflect and reassess. That alone is a success.

The truth is, you are the driver of your career. Nobody else will steer it for you. Taking full ownership of your path allows you to:

- Recognize when it's time for a change

- Align your work with your values and strengths

- Seek opportunities that truly fit your goals and vision

I've experienced this cycle multiple times in my career. Each time, I reached a point where I had achieved what I set out to do and felt it was time to challenge myself in a new environment, with new possibilities.
The key is not to remain stuck just because something once worked. Growth requires forward motion.

This is just the beginning. You've already made meaningful progress by investing in yourself. Now it's time to build on that momentum. We've created additional sections and resources to help you continue elevating your career and expanding your capabilities.

Stay curious. Stay proactive. And remember: the next step could be the one that transforms your career.

SECTION 2

EMOTIONAL INTELLIGENCE MASTERY
FOR RISING PROFESSIONALS
By Hiba Tanvir

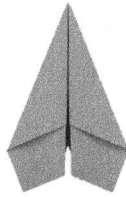

CHAPTER 5

No, It's Not Fluff: The Hard Truth About Emotional Intelligence

When you hear the term *emotional intelligence*, what comes to mind? A new-age theory about emotions? A strategy for playing nice at work? Or just a way to be more agreeable?

Let's pause here. As soon as we hear words like "emotion" or "emotional," many of us imagine someone drowning in feelings and getting sad, dramatic, or out of control. The truth is that emotions make people uncomfortable. But why?

Being uncomfortable with emotions is like being uncomfortable with air. Emotions are integral to our existence. They shape every thought, every decision. Yet, for centuries, we've misunderstood and even vilified them, treating emotions as weak, irrational, or something to suppress.

This discomfort has created a deep divide between two core aspects of humanity: emotion and intelligence. Many of us are conditioned to believe these qualities are mutually exclusive. Society often suggests that if you're emotional, you can't possibly be intelligent, and if you're intelligent, you must suppress your emotions.

But what if that's wrong? What if I told you that the smartest thing you can do is embrace and understand your emotions?

Let's unpack what emotional intelligence truly means and why it's the skill set you need to thrive in today's world.

First, we need to reconsider *emotion*. By definition, an emotion is:

- An internal experience of mood or feeling that influences thoughts and behaviors

- A psychological and physiological reaction to a stimulus, involving subjective experience and outward expression

- From the moment we're born, emotions help us survive. For instance:

- *Joy* appears in early smiles, first reflexive, then social, helping babies bond with caregivers.

- *Distress* shows through crying when needs aren't met.

- *Interest* is seen when babies focus on faces or new stimuli in their environment.

These early emotions are nature's way of ensuring we not only survive but also connect, learn, and thrive. So, why do we vilify emotions? Stereotypes tell us:

- Emotional people are sensitive, caring, irrational, and impractical.

- Intelligent people are smart, stoic, practical, and goal-oriented.

Do you see the challenge? We've been taught to believe you can't be both emotional and intelligent. This mindset has fueled gender bias for centuries, casting "emotional" as a feminine trait and "intelligent" as a masculine one, perpetuating patriarchy and limiting everyone in the process. In reality, emotions aren't a liability. They're a strength. They are a form of innate intelligence designed to guide us through life's highs and lows.

Now, let's turn to *intelligence.*

Intelligence is defined as the ability to acquire, understand, and apply knowledge and skills to solve problems, adapt to new situations, and think critically and creatively.

It's time to reframe what intelligence really means.

True intelligence isn't about divorcing yourself from emotion. It's about using emotion as a tool to deepen your thinking, sharpen your decisions, and strengthen your relationships.

Think of some of the world's most effective leaders—Mother Teresa, Nelson Mandela, or Jeff Bezos. What do they have in common? Not just intellect. They possess exceptional interpersonal skills, deep self-awareness, and the ability to connect with others. These are hallmarks of emotional intelligence.

So, what is emotional intelligence? Let's keep it simple:

Emotional intelligence is the ability to recognize, understand, label, express, and regulate emotions in yourself and others to create synergy and healthy relationships.

It's a skillset that transforms both your career and your personal life too. When you invest in emotional intelligence, you set yourself up for:

- Career success, promotions, and higher earning potential

- Deeper, more fulfilling relationships with partners, children, family, and colleagues

Research backs this up. *TalentSmart* tested emotional intelligence alongside 33 other workplace skills and found it's the strongest predictor of performance, accounting for 58% of success across all job types.

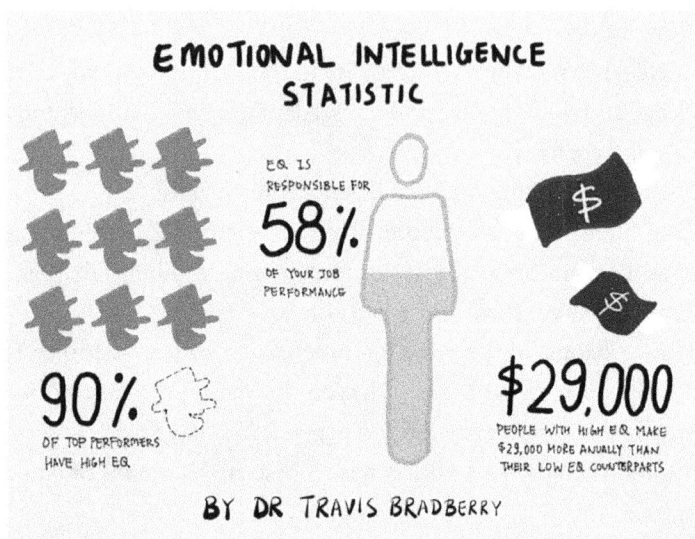

EMOTIONAL INTELLIGENCE STATISTIC

EQ IS RESPONSIBLE FOR 58% OF YOUR JOB PERFORMANCE

90% OF TOP PERFORMERS HAVE HIGH EQ

$29,000 PEOPLE WITH HIGH EQ MAKE $29,000 MORE ANNUALLY THAN THEIR LOW EQ COUNTERPARTS

BY DR TRAVIS BRADBERRY

Think of someone who was "difficult" in your life, perhaps a boss, a coworker, or even a family member. How would you describe them?

Common responses include erratic, selfish, bossy, rude, and inconsiderate.

Now, think of someone who inspired or supported you. How would you describe them?

Chances are, words like compassionate, intelligent, kind, responsible, or energetic come to mind.

What's the difference? Emotional intelligence. The people who challenge us often lack it. The ones who uplift and empower us? They tend to excel at it.

A New Way Forward

Long before artificial intelligence (AI), emotional intelligence *(EI)* was the ultimate flex—the skill that determined the success of leaders, teams, and even empires. The good news? This skillset isn't reserved for the elite. It's available to everyone, including you.

But here's the catch: there are no quick fixes. Raising your EQ (emotional quotient) requires commitment, practice, and self-reflection. Like any significant journey, it starts with small steps but leads to transformational results.

So, are you ready to embrace both emotion and intelligence? By the end of the next few chapters, you'll have the tools to elevate your EQ and use it to thrive in every area of your life.

Let's get started!

Reflection Questions:

- Do you see *emotion* and *intelligence* as complementary or opposing concepts? Why?

- What stereotypes about being "emotional" or "intelligent" have you encountered in your personal or professional life?

- Reflect on a time when you felt judged for being too emotional or too rational. How did that impact you?

- What would you like to improve about your relationships at work or home through emotional intelligence?

CHAPTER 6

The Emotional Edge: Why EQ is Your Ultimate Superpower

I'm often asked what sparked my interest in studying emotional intelligence. The truth is, long before I even knew the term existed, I was deeply attuned to the emotions and moods of those around me. As a child, I was highly sensitive to tone of voice, facial expressions, and subtle shifts in energy. Being a naturally peaceful and harmony-seeking person, I subconsciously made it my mission to maintain peace by avoiding conflict at all costs. I did everything in my power not to upset those around me, often diffusing tension before it could escalate.

Was I being emotionally intelligent? Not at all. In fact, I was doing quite the opposite.

That pattern led to emotional burnout, anxiety, and a habit of prioritizing others' comfort over my own well-being. I became an empath who was easily walked over by those lacking empathy themselves. My desire for peace and conflict-avoidant nature turned into a vulnerability, allowing others to manipulate me.

What was missing? I was likable, agreeable, and approachable—qualities that served me well both personally and professionally. But I lacked two critical elements: discernment and boundaries.

This ties back to a common stereotype we discussed in the previous chapter: many of us hesitate to engage with our emotions because we fear they will make us vulnerable. We worry that acknowledging our feelings will lead to exploitation or a loss of respect.

But true emotional intelligence isn't about being agreeable or suppressing emotions. It's about understanding, managing, and leveraging them for personal and professional success.

Let's break down the four core components of emotional intelligence.

1. Self-Awareness: The Foundation of Emotional Intelligence

Self-awareness is the ability to understand your strengths, weaknesses, triggers, and motivators. It is the foundation of emotional intelligence, and without it, real growth simply isn't possible.

I emphasize self-awareness in all my talks and workshops because it's both the most challenging and the most transformative skill. It requires deep reflection and the willingness to sit with discomfort. If you don't actively develop self-awareness, your ability to enhance your emotional intelligence will be significantly limited.

Developing self-awareness

Here are three powerful actions that you can take right now to enhance your self-awareness:

- List three of your strengths.

- Identify up to four weaknesses or areas for growth.

- Reflect further and add three more areas for improvement.

When I lead this activity during workshops, I can feel the energy shift in the room. People breeze through listing their strengths because those are easy. They're the qualities we're praised for and proud of. But when it's time to name weaknesses, discomfort sets in.

Why? Because we live in a world that glorifies strength and success while urging us to hide our weaknesses. Acknowledging them feels like admitting we are *less than*—less valuable, less capable, less desirable.

But here's the truth: your growth, your emotional intelligence, and your leadership potential lie in your self-awareness.

If you take away only one thing from this chapter, let it be this: Invest in your self-awareness. Get comfortable with the discomfort of identifying, owning, and working on your areas of growth.

2. Self-Management: Turning Awareness into Action

Self-awareness is powerful, yet it's only the beginning. To realize its full potential, you need self-management: the ability to regulate your emotions and behaviors in a way that serves your personal and professional goals.

Let me give you an example.

James, a client of mine, once told me:

"I'm very self-aware. I know I have an anger problem. I get triggered easily and lose my temper. But at least I own it! Unlike others who pretend they're fine, I'm honest. I just tell people to leave me alone when I'm in that mood. It's simple."

Is James self-aware? You could argue, yes, he acknowledges his anger issues. But listen closely to what comes next: he offloads responsibility onto others. He expects the world to accommodate his behavior instead of working to change it.

This is where self-management comes in.

Self-awareness without self-management is often just manipulation and control. Beware of individuals who use their "self-awareness" as an excuse for inappropriate behavior. True emotional intelligence requires accountability. It's not enough to recognize your weaknesses. You must take responsibility for managing them.

Developing Self-Management

If you recognize a challenge within yourself, ask:

- What steps can I take to regulate this emotion?

- What activities, places, or people help me feel grounded?

- What is my personal definition of "home" or comfort?

For example, a client once told me she experiences severe anxiety during the holiday season. This shows self-awareness. Self-management, however, means creating an action plan to navigate those emotions, perhaps by setting boundaries, scheduling downtime, or surrounding herself with supportive people.

3. Social Awareness: Expanding Beyond the Self

While self-awareness and self-management focus inward, social awareness shifts the lens outward. It is the ability to read a room, understand and navigate social dynamics, and sense the emotions of others.

Many people are drawn to emotional intelligence because they want to improve their relationships. But a common misstep is approaching EI with the goal of changing others rather than working on themselves.

This is a cardinal sin in emotional intelligence. As long as you are focused on fixing others, you will struggle to develop your own EQ.

At the heart of social awareness are two key forces: empathy and compassion.

- *Empathy*: the ability to step into someone else's shoes and understand their emotions.

- *Compassion:* taking that understanding and turning it into action.

Example:

A friend is grieving the loss of a parent.

- *Empathy*: You listen, validate their feelings, and share your own experiences with loss.

- *Compassion*: You go beyond words, perhaps by cooking them a meal, checking in on them, or offering practical support.

Empathy is understanding. Compassion is action.

4. Relationship Building

The last component of emotional intelligence is the ability to build and maintain strong, healthy relationships. This requires communication, teamwork, conflict resolution, and influence.

Example:

Two coworkers are in a heated disagreement. Rather than taking sides or ignoring the issue, you step in as a mediator, encouraging open dialogue and guiding them toward common ground.

Many people turn to emotional intelligence because they want to be heard, respected, and treated better. But true transformation happens when we stop seeking quick fixes and instead commit to consistent self-reflection, embrace critical feedback, and practice empathy and compassion, especially when it's uncomfortable.

When I think of relationship building, I think of my parents, Shamsa and Tanvir. They embodied real leadership through their actions. They never sought recognition but focused solely on uplifting others. Whether supporting family or those who worked for them, they built a reputation for dependability and generosity. For them, success was never a solo pursuit. It was about bringing others along on the journey.

Decades later, they are reaping the rewards of that selfless investment, receiving respect, love, and friendships that have endured for over 50 years. Their legacy is a testament to the power of intentional, heart-led relationship-building, the kind that stands the test of time.

The transformative journey of developing your emotional intelligence isn't something you can complete in isolation. You won't become emotionally intelligent by meditating alone on a mountaintop. True growth happens in the messy, unpredictable, and deeply human moments of connection. It's through real interactions, especially when frustration flares, stress mounts, or misunderstandings arise, that you refine your self-awareness, self-management, social awareness, and relationship-building skills.

That's why your emotional well-being depends on having a tribe, a circle of people who support you, offer honest feedback, and help you see yourself more clearly. My sister, Sabiha, models this balance beautifully in both her personal and professional life. She taught me that intelligence must remain tethered to emotion, just as emotion must stay anchored in reason.

I wouldn't have developed my own emotional intelligence without the support of the extraordinary women in my life. They honored my emotions but also challenged me to rise higher, give more, and do more with them. Those women know who they are, and I am forever grateful for them, for their emotions, and for their intelligence.

Why Emotional Intelligence Is a "Must-Have" in Business

You might think, "This makes sense for personal relationships, but why should leaders and organizations invest in emotional intelligence?"

I'm glad you asked. The data speaks for itself:

- *Employee Performance:* Studies show a strong correlation exists between EI and higher job performance (Tandfonline, 2024).

- *Leadership Effectiveness*: Emotionally intelligent leaders improve team productivity and outcomes (PMC, 2024).

- *Employee Engagement & Productivity*: EI-driven workplaces experience higher engagement and efficiency (Niagara Institute, 2024).

- *Customer Satisfaction*: Companies with emotionally intelligent teams report stronger customer loyalty (Niagara Institute, 2024).

- *Stress & Burnout Reduction*: EI helps employees manage stress and avoid burnout (PMC, 2019).

Unlike many business investments that demand significant time and financial resources to deliver ROI, the benefits of EI are immediate. In fact, just by reading this chapter, you've already taken the most important step: the first step.

Emotional Frequency and Energy in Emotional Intelligence

I first learned about emotional frequency from my friend, Amy Thurman, NYT bestselling author of *Finding My Hero Within*. Amy shared a powerful insight: each emotion carries its own energy, frequency, and vibration. I'd heard that before, but what fascinated me was her revelation that emotions follow the color pattern of a rainbow.

After years of suffering through undiagnosed, excruciating pain, Amy could have easily drowned in despair, anger, and fear. But instead, she made a conscious choice—every single day—to climb one rung higher on the emotional frequency ladder, gradually moving toward joy, gratitude, and healing.

This mirrors the principles found on Dr. David Hawkins' *Emotional Frequency Scale*, which maps how different emotions vibrate at different energy levels. As you develop your emotional intelligence, you'll begin to shift from low-frequency emotions—like shame and guilt—towards higher states of peace and joy. It won't happen overnight. It may not even happen over the course of a year. But it *will* happen, one step and one emotion at a time. (See chart below.)

Map of Consciousness
Developed By David R. Hawkins

	Name of Level	Energetic Log	Predominant Emotional State	View of Life	God-view	Process
Spiritual Paradigm	Enlightenment	700-1000	Ineffable	Is	Self	Pure Consciousness
	Peace	600	Bliss	Perfect	All-Being	Illumination
	Joy	540	Serenity	Complete	One	Transfiguration
	Love	500	Reverence	Benign	Loving	Revelation
Reason & Integrity	Reason	400	Understanding	Meaningful	Wise	Abstraction
	Acceptance	350	Forgiveness	Harmonious	Merciful	Transcendence
	Willingness	310	Optimism	Hopeful	Inspiring	Intention
	Neutrality	250	Trust	Satisfactory	Enabling	Release
	Courage	200	Affirmation	Feasible	Permitting	Empowerment
Survival Paradigm	Pride	175	Scorn	Demanding	Indifferent	Inflation
	Anger	150	Hate	Antagonistic	Vengeful	Aggression
	Desire	125	Craving	Disappointing	Denying	Enslavement
	Fear	100	Anxiety	Frightening	Punitive	Withdrawal
	Grief	75	Regret	Tragic	Disdainful	Despondency
	Apathy	50	Despair	Hopeless	Condemning	Abdication
	Guilt	30	Blame	Evil	Vindictive	Destruction
	Shame	20	Humiliation	Miserable	Despising	Elimination

Figure 1. Map of Consciousness chart. From Scott, "How to Measure Consciousness With the Map of Consciousness," Life-Long Learner, 2025.

Reflection Questions:

- On a scale of 1–5, rate yourself in each EI component. Have a mentor and a close friend rate you as well. Reflect on the patterns.

- Think of a coworker facing personal difficulties. How could you show empathy? How could you show compassion?

- Which emotional intelligence benefit resonated most with you? What's your motivation for improving your EQ?

Take a moment to reflect on up to four people in your life who can truly support your emotional intelligence growth. These should be individuals you trust, people whose honesty you value and whose feedback you're willing to receive, even when it's uncomfortable.

Who in your circle challenges you to be more self-aware? To manage your emotions effectively? To build stronger, more authentic relationships? Identify them, appreciate them, and lean into their guidance.

Now, take a moment to review the emotional frequency chart. Which emotional states do you find yourself experiencing most often? Pay attention to the corresponding views of life and any patterns or insights that emerge. Then, set a realistic intention to move just one or two steps up the emotional scale. What specific actions or mindset shifts could support that upward movement? Even small, consistent changes can create powerful emotional momentum.

Final Thought

Raising your emotional intelligence is like decluttering your mind. It's a commitment to removing emotional excess, organizing your thoughts, and gaining clarity in your relationships.

The more you invest in EI, the more every area of your life begins to transform from the inside out.

CHAPTER 7
The AI Era: Why EQ is Your Competitive Advantage

I was having trouble with my brand-new dryer. It would run for a bit and then flash an error message. I googled possible solutions and tried fixing it, but the issue kept returning and moving me down a few rungs on the emotional spectrum.

Eventually, I did what I dreaded the most: called customer service. My problem was unique. I was frustrated and didn't want to talk to an artificial system, no matter how human it pretended to be. In fact, the more human the system tried to act, the more irritated I became.

Why? Because when we experience strong emotions, whether low-frequency or high-frequency, we crave real human conversation and connection. So, I wanted to speak with a perfectly imperfect human who could listen and walk me through a solution. Maybe the AI system could provide the same answers, but I craved human connection.

As we navigate the AI era, many of us are simultaneously learning, exploring, and embracing its vast potential. But much like a child who unwraps a mountain of exciting, tech-driven birthday gifts—remote-controlled toys, cutting-edge gadgets, and futuristic innovations—what they truly seek at the end of the day is the warmth of a parent's hug. Similarly, despite AI's advancements, what we ultimately crave is human connection.

Unlike those who fear AI will replace human communication and render many jobs obsolete, I believe the opposite is true. AI will illuminate what makes us irreplaceably human and elevate the value of our relationships and emotional intelligence.

In the AI era, many jobs are becoming redundant, and this trend will continue. But the human positions that remain will demand a higher level of "humanness." Organizations won't just be hiring for skills; they'll be seeking people who can navigate uncertainty, lead with empathy, and elevate others to higher-frequency emotions. As discussed in the previous chapter, the ability to build strong, emotionally intelligent relationships is more than a soft skill; it's a competitive edge.

The buzzwords dominating organizational culture today, such as authenticity, vulnerability, empathy, are all emotional states being recognized and rewarded. But they're not just checkboxes. To be authentic, you must be self-aware, willing to examine your blind spots, and courageous enough to grow. Vulnerability, when rooted in self-awareness, naturally extends into relationship-building. Empathy, as discussed earlier, remains a cornerstone of social awareness.

If there's ever been a time when emotional intelligence matters most and is the most profitable investment, it's NOW. To thrive in an AI-driven world, you must not view AI as a threat or competition. Instead, you must reflect and re-evaluate what makes you uniquely human and dare to embrace those qualities.

For example, rather than allowing AI to draft your next email or LinkedIn post, write it yourself. Managers, leaders, and clients are already flooded with AI-generated perfection. Set yourself apart by embracing your humanity and letting your imperfections show. In today's world, authenticity is the new green flag.

A recent Gallup study featured in the *Global Leadership Report: What Followers Want* highlights that hope is the most critical quality followers seek in their leaders. Surveying participants across 52 countries, representing 76% of the global adult population and 86% of the world's GDP, Gallup asked them to identify a leader who positively influenced their daily lives. The findings revealed that 56% of the respondents associated hope with positive leadership, surpassing other attributes such as trust (33%), compassion (7%), and stability (4%).

The study also showed a strong correlation between leadership qualities and individual well-being. Among those who did not associate hope with their leaders, only 33% were classified as thriving, while 9% were suffering. In contrast, when leaders were seen as a source of hope, the thriving ratio increased to 38% while suffering dropped to 6%. This suggests that leaders who inspire hope significantly enhance the well-being of their followers.

These findings reinforce a timeless truth: no matter how much the world changes, people still long for leaders who offer hope, trust, compassion, and stability. In turbulent times, hope in leaders keeps us moving forward. It makes the world feel less chaotic. It provides psychological safety. It creates belonging.

Emotionally intelligent leaders have hope in themselves and know how to instill it in others. When you reverse-engineer hope, you'll find it requires mastery of the four components of emotional intelligence: self-awareness, self-management, social awareness, and relationship-building.

Over coffee one day, my friend and colleague Robert Hunt shared the heart of his work as an executive coach with REF. He spoke clearly and confidently, but I listened beyond his words and frameworks to grasp what he truly offers.

At its core, Robert gives leaders something invaluable: hope. It is the hope that they can grow, lead with purpose, and achieve meaningful impact. However, he doesn't stop there. Hope without a plan is just a warm sentiment. Robert equips leaders with practical strategies to turn that hope into real results.

That conversation made me reflect on my own journey. When I founded Hope Kitchen, it wasn't just about creating a home-based catering business for women in crisis. It was about helping them reclaim their dignity and self-worth. Many of these women had been overlooked, their potential unseen. But once they were given the chance to work, earn, and build a future, they began to transform. Some moved from low-income housing to owning homes. I don't take credit for their success; they did the hard work. But I gave them something they hadn't received in a long time. I gave them hope.

Emotional intelligence in leadership isn't just about managing emotions. It's about recognizing the unspoken needs of those we lead and inspiring them toward growth. Hope is one of the most powerful tools a leader can offer. But true leadership goes beyond offering encouragement; it requires action, guidance, and belief in the potential of others.

When I reflect on the most successful initiatives I've led, such as *Hope Kitchen* for struggling women, the *Man Up* program for youth in Africa, and emotional well-being classes at a senior living facility, one power connects them all: hope. I believed in the people I served. And because I had hope in them, I could give it to them.

One senior at the living facility once told me,

"When we see you walk in with your radiant energy, you give us hope that some young person still finds us worthy of their time."

So, ask yourself: What are you doing as a leader—at home, in your community, or at work—to give hope to the people around you? Because leadership isn't about a title. You don't have to be a leader to give hope. But when you're giving it, you become one.

And remember this: artificial intelligence cannot give someone hope. It can assist. It can optimize. It can even predict. But it cannot connect to the human soul the way another human can. Humans don't look to machines for hope. They look to each other, especially to those willing to lead with heart. Be that human being.

Reflection Questions:

- Challenge yourself daily to send at least one email or write a social media post without using ChatGPT or any other AI tool. Embrace the fear of imperfection.

- Write a handwritten note to someone who has positively affected your life. Notice how much more physical and emotional effort it takes. These are the muscles we need to keep exercising.

- Practice what you would say to a colleague who seems to lose hope in himself. Perhaps he has been struggling at work and feels like a failure. The better you become at instilling hope in others, the sharper your emotional intelligence and leadership skills will grow.

SECTION 3

STRESS MANAGEMENT 101
FOR HIGH ACHIEVERS
By Donya Smida

CHAPTER 8

Stress 101: What You Need to Know

Whenever I introduce myself as a stress management coach, I get asked the same question: "Oh, what brought you here? Have you been in the health sector before?"

This question always made me uncomfortable because I didn't have a tidy, one-sentence answer like, "It's my passion to help people" or "That's my calling" or "Yeah, I studied psychology."

None of those felt true. None of those was the real reason I became a stress management coach. So, I started digging deeper.

What actually pushed me to leave a 17-year corporate career and step into coaching? What was the turning point?

Of course, change doesn't come from a single event, comment or moment of reflection. It's usually the result of many small moments building over time.

Still, I was determined to trace it back. I kept asking myself,

"When did I decide things would never be the same again?"

"What did I need to experience to finally say, 'I'm meant for something else?'"

And then it hit me. I knew exactly where it started. It was during one of those routine, scripted, and soul-numbing events we all know too well in corporate life: the annual performance review. Mine took place in January 2021.

I'd flown from Tunisia to Malta to meet with my boss and colleagues. Normally, I enjoyed the trip. It was a short break from home, a chance to reconnect with the team, and a few days to recharge before returning with a fresh set of goals and targets for the year ahead. After 17 years, I knew what to expect. These reviews were usually positive. Encouraging, even. They gave me a boost of motivation.

But this time was going to be different.

The meeting began as expected. We reviewed my objectives, and my boss seemed genuinely pleased with my accomplishments.

"You had a successful year," he said. "You hit your targets, and I appreciate your commitment to growing the portfolio."

I nodded, listened, and responded professionally. But something inside me felt off. I was emotionally detached. While I told myself I should feel proud, I didn't. It all felt...routine. Expected. I was just doing my job. I wanted the meeting to end because talking about myself didn't interest me anymore. I would've rather gotten back to work to finish what was on my plate.

Then, my boss made a comment I didn't see coming:

"I'm happy overall, but I'm disappointed you didn't focus more on networking and building connections, Donya. That's something you need to work on."

In that moment, my stomach dropped. I kept a composed expression and asked follow-up questions, but inside, I was unraveling. The point he raised wasn't even that significant, especially considering everything else I'd accomplished. Still, his words hit me hard. I could feel tears pressing behind my eyes.

It's okay, I told myself. It's just a small comment. *Don't make it a big deal. You'll be fine.*

But a louder voice pushed through:

He's disappointed in you. You failed. You should have done more.

When the meeting finally ended, I was barely holding it together. I left his office and ran into some colleagues in the hallway. They took one look at me and asked,

"What happened in there? You look like something terrible just happened."

I couldn't explain it. Nothing had really gone wrong. The meeting had been mostly positive. My boss hadn't yelled, criticized, or embarrassed me. And that made it even worse. How could one small comment wreck me like this?

It took me a month to recover. During that time, the same question kept haunting me: *Why did this hurt so much?*

Eventually, I came to a profound realization. The meeting wasn't painful because of what my boss said. It was painful because it forced me to face a truth I had buried for too long: I was successful yet miserable.

For years, I had shouldered high-stakes responsibilities. I managed a multimillion-dollar portfolio, led a large team, and handled high-stakes work in international organizations. My role demanded precision, composure, and constant results. I took pride in juggling it all and always showing up prepared, delivering results, and keeping everything under control.

But behind the scenes, the weight of it all was crushing me. Every decision I made carried consequences, and every mistake felt unforgivable. And on top of that, I was a mother of three, balancing early morning flights, meetings with government officials, and late nights at the office with school pickups, homework, and family dinners. Some days, I felt like a superhero; on other days, I felt like I was barely surviving.

By the age of 41, I had made every choice in my life with intention: my career, my partner, my family, my professional shifts from engineering to HR to management. And yet, I couldn't enjoy any of it. I couldn't feel peace. I couldn't rest.

I was constantly stressed, annoyed, and exhausted.

Yes, I could "handle it all." But at what cost?

Stress had hijacked my well-being and stolen my sense of fulfillment.

For a long time, I ignored the wake-up calls. Missing a flight after a chaotic work trip, forgetting to drop my child off at kindergarten, only realizing she was still with me when we pulled into the office, were just a few.

But that one moment during the annual review?

It wasn't just feedback.

It was the alarm that forced me to start asking hard questions.

Why do I accept stress as a given?

Why do I wear it like a badge of honor?

I knew I wasn't alone in this. I saw it everywhere: in my team, across industries, and among friends, people juggling careers, families, and personal goals, all while treating chronic stress as normal.

I realized I didn't want to just survive stress. I wanted something more.

My coaching journey started in January 2021. It started with a hunger to understand myself better. I devoured books on personal growth. I consulted coaches and mentors. I enrolled in courses, webinars, and masterminds about spiritual learning, self-development, stress management, and life coaching. Those lessons changed everything.

They helped me break free from the persistent sense of unfulfillment rooted in stress and unrealistic expectations. I learned how to manage pressure without letting every comment or event throw me off balance.

What began as a personal rescue mission turned into a calling.

When I learned that 83% of employees in the U.S. reported feeling stressed, I asked myself whether stress could be reduced without sacrificing ambition, achievement, or success. I believed the answer was yes.

And so, I embarked on a mission to prove that success didn't have to come at the cost of well-being, showing that individuals can thrive professionally *and* personally without compromise.

In 2022, I became a certified stress management coach and shortly thereafter launched my business. By the end of 2023, I left my corporate job to become a full-time coach, speaker, and trainer.

In this section of the book, I'll share what I've learned not just as a coach, but as someone who has lived it. Someone who's felt the pressure, faced the doubts, and found a way through.

This journey, which began with a single comment during that annual review, is meant to inspire you to pause, reflect, and get started on your own path to managing stress and reclaiming balance in your life.

Because here's the truth: stress is inevitable. But it doesn't have to control you. You have the power to shift your relationship with it. You can lead, achieve, and *still* have space to breathe.

This book is not about quick fixes or temporary relief. It's about building sustainable strategies that reduce stress and create a life of harmony, clarity, and purpose. Just as I did, you'll gain tools and insights that empower you to respond to stress instead of being ruled by it. You'll learn to navigate challenges with resilience and self-awareness. You'll discover how to manage stress effectively, rather than allowing it to control you. This journey is about regaining control, protecting your energy, and thriving without compromise.

How to Build a Supportive Mindset

Let's talk about how your thoughts can either amplify or reduce stress and how to focus on what truly matters. By learning to respond rather than react, you'll begin to see stress not as an enemy, but as an opportunity for personal growth.

But before we dive in, what exactly is stress?

The World Health Organization (WHO) defines stress as "a state of worry or mental tension caused by a difficult situation. Stress is a natural human response that prompts us to address challenges and threats."

Now, I can hear you saying, "But Donya, stress is natural! There's nothing I can do about it!"

Well...yes and no.

Yes, stress is a natural response to tension, but you have the power to decide what counts as tension. What feels overwhelming to one person might seem completely manageable to someone else. It all comes down to perception.

Perception Is Key

This is where psychologist Richard Lazarus's *Cognitive Appraisal Theory of Stress* comes in. It's one of the most influential psychological frameworks for understanding how your thoughts shape your experience of stress.

According to Lazarus, when we face a situation, your brain runs two quick assessments:

- *Primary Appraisal:* Is this a threat or an opportunity?

  If you perceive the situation as a threat, stress is likely to follow.

- *Secondary Appraisal:* Can I handle this?

  If you believe you can cope, the stress diminishes. If you feel powerless, it intensifies.

Ultimately, your mind decides whether something is stressful based on those two appraisals. And your lived experiences, values, and belief systems shape those assessments. In short, stress isn't just about what's happening around you; it's about how you internalize it.

Your mindset and how you process your thoughts are critical in determining whether stress becomes a paralyzing weight or a manageable challenge.

Take the example of a corporate restructuring email sent to employees. Emma, a senior manager, reads it and immediately panics.

This means layoffs. My job could be at risk. What if I lose my team?

Her primary appraisal identifies a threat. This perception triggers stress, anxiety, and fear. Then, in her secondary appraisal, she doubts her coping abilities.

I don't have the skills to navigate this. I won't be able to adapt.

Her stress skyrockets. Frustration and helplessness follow.

Leila, another senior manager, receives the same email. She also sees the change as a threat but reframes it as an opportunity.

This could be a chance for me to grow, lead through uncertainty, and make an impact.

Her confidence in her ability to manage the challenge softens the stress.

Cathy, a new hire, perceives the situation as a positive change.

I've handled transitions before. I can leverage my skills and network to stay ahead.

With a high belief in her capability, her reaction is proactive and calm. The difference among these three women? Their mindset.

Research shows that individuals with a supportive mindset—those who approach challenges with clarity, resilience, and a proactive outlook—experience significantly less emotional and physical strain than those who feel powerless or reactive to their circumstances.

My message to you is to think of stress as a signal, a cue that something in your life needs attention. The key isn't to eliminate stress but to learn how to manage it, so it no longer dominates your thoughts, emotions, and well-being.

How do you build a supportive mindset? It all starts with self-awareness, the cornerstone of effective stress management.

According to research in emotional intelligence by Dr. Daniel Goleman, individuals with high self-awareness can identify their stress triggers early and manage them effectively, reducing emotional and physical strain. When you understand why something affects you, you gain the power to respond instead of reacting.

The 5S Process: From Reaction to Reflection

Do you remember the story at the beginning of the previous chapter and how my supervisor's words, "I'm disappointed," cut so deeply during my annual review? I began to unravel that moment not by analyzing his intent, but by exploring my reaction. Instead of playing the victim, blaming him for being too blunt or insensitive, I realized the hurt wasn't about what he said; it was about the story I told myself about the meaning of that experience.

Although I didn't yet have a structured process for self-reflection, I began questioning myself. That moment sparked a personal breakthrough, which eventually led me to develop a powerful mindset tool for my clients: the 5S Process.

The 5S Process is an essential tool for developing a supportive mindset. It enables you to become aware of your thoughts and emotions, so you can break free from patterns that hold you back and take intentional steps toward lasting growth.

Step 1: Stop Blaming Others

Blame keeps you stuck. It focuses your energy on things you can't control. Stress loosens its grip when you accept that the issue isn't the other person's behavior but *your response* to it.

Step 2: Stop Making Up Stories

As long as you keep spinning stories to justify your emotions, you will never be able to manage them. By stories, I mean dwelling on accusations, trying to rationalize what the other person did, and making excuses for how you feel.

Step 3: Start Identifying the Triggers

Ask yourself: What was triggered? Was it your need for control? Your desire to be seen as perfect? Your longing to feel valued? Pinpointing what part of you felt attacked will give you clarity and power.

Step 4: Start Uncovering Limiting Beliefs

Behind every emotional trigger is a belief. Do you believe that you have to be perfect to succeed? That working harder than everyone else is the only way to achieve? That being liked means always being agreeable? Identifying the belief behind the triggers is a game-changer. Once you recognize it, you can begin rewriting it.

Step 5: Stop the Pattern

Once you identify what's triggering you and uncover the limiting belief or story behind it, you can intentionally choose a different response. Stop letting that pattern dictate your reactions and begin creating new ways of thinking that empower you instead of draining you.

Be honest with yourself and uncover the truth. It might be related to self-esteem, self-confidence, self-worth, or something similar.

Going through these five steps myself wasn't easy. But with deep honesty, I finally recognized a truth about myself: I wanted people to like me. Unconsciously, that desire controlled how I reacted to situations. My emotions were often tied to what others thought of me. The more I reflected, the clearer it became: this need for validation was placing unnecessary pressure on me, pushing me to take on more and more things to gain approval.

Working on my self-worth was the next logical step. By putting in time and effort, I became less triggered by external factors and less sensitive to how others perceived me. That was a huge step forward. I was no longer caught in the emotional rollercoaster of seeking approval, and I started to feel a sense of relief.

But as I peeled back this layer, I uncovered a more profound truth: there were still parts of me that had not been explored and new areas to work on. I realized that real change doesn't come from a single breakthrough. It's an ongoing process, like peeling an onion. The work never stops, but the relief and clarity that come with every step forward make the effort worthwhile.

Without doing this inner work, you'll never find the purpose and direction that are essential for cultivating a supportive mindset.

Finding Purpose and Direction

When I was a senior executive, I was fully wrapped up in my role. I identified as the leader, the manager, the one with clear professional goals and a career-driven purpose. That influenced everything I did. So, when someone from the outside, like my boss, would express doubts or criticize me, it hit me hard. It didn't feel like feedback about my work; it felt like a direct attack on who I was.

I couldn't separate my goals and sense of purpose from my job. So, when my boss said, "I'm disappointed," my brain went straight to: *I've failed. I've failed at my professional goals, which means I've failed at my purpose.*

That was a wake-up call for me. It made me realize something important: I lacked a bigger purpose, something that was truly mine. Sure, I had goals for my kids, for my team, and for the organization. But at the core, I didn't have a personal sense of purpose outside of my work or my role as a mom. That realization came as a bit of a shock.

I had spent so much energy focusing outward that I had forgotten about Donya—the person beneath all the roles and expectations.

That was a second turning point for me. It prompted me to discover a purpose that was solely my own.

Without a clear sense of direction, you're constantly searching for something, but not really knowing what you're looking for. You might be busy checking off tasks, responding to emails, or meeting deadlines, but deep down, there's a sense of being lost. You're working hard, but it doesn't feel meaningful because you're not sure what you're truly working toward.

That kind of confusion creates stress. When your purpose is unclear, you default to external pressures. You chase roles, approval, and productivity without a personal *why*. It's like driving aimlessly without a destination. But once you do discover your purpose, it's like plugging the right coordinates into your GPS. You start moving with intention, and everything becomes clearer.

A 2019 study published in the *Journal of Happiness Studies* found something powerful: people with clear life goals show higher resilience and lower levels of stress, even in tough situations. Why? Because when you know your purpose, challenges stop feeling like insurmountable barriers. They become stepping stones for growth.

Let me be clear: getting clear about your purpose doesn't mean abandoning your professional goals. They still matter, and they still help you grow. But once you have a strong sense of purpose, your career no longer defines *who* you are; it becomes a vehicle to express who you are becoming. Those goals serve the bigger picture rather than shaping your identity.

With that clarity, everything will start to fall into place. You will feel more grounded, more focused, and better equipped to handle life's challenges.

Building a Supportive Identity

A supportive identity is another essential tool in your arsenal for building a resilient and empowering mindset.

Carol Dweck's research on self-identity highlights how our self-perception influences our ability to manage stress. Identity plays a crucial role. When you see yourself as capable of growth and adaptation, you're more likely to face stressors with resilience instead of fear. By cultivating a growth-oriented identity, you can reframe stress as manageable and even beneficial, boosting both your well-being and performance.

For years, I defined myself by external achievements: titles, positions, and others' expectations. I saw myself as the leader, the manager, the mom, and the wife. But once I began focusing on my own goals and purpose, I realized that the identity I had built didn't reflect all aspects of my life—professional, social, emotional, and personal. It was fragmented. Misaligned.

I needed to evolve. I needed to redefine my identity in a way that aligned with my life purpose and embraced all parts of who I am while helping me manage expectations and stress. A growth-oriented identity doesn't mean becoming someone new. It means becoming *more* of who you truly are.

True peace and self-worth come from embracing yourself as you are. But your identity isn't set in stone; it's constantly shaped by your beliefs, experiences, and aspirations. When you choose an identity aligned with your values, it helps reduce stress by bringing clarity and purpose.

Seeing your identity as fluid empowers you to evolve, grow, and unlock new possibilities while staying true to who you are at your core.

I realized I needed to choose an identity that wasn't based on what I *assumed* others thought of me. Instead of being confined by old perceptions or external expectations, I chose to build an identity rooted in my values, my goals, and my sense of purpose. One that would empower me and bring me joy, free from stress and the weight of others' judgments.

Here's the identity I've chosen to embrace:

I believe in education, freedom of choice, and equality. I'm committed to supporting others' growth and making a meaningful impact. With this in mind, I've embraced the identity of a leader, an educator, and a change maker; someone who uplifts, inspires, and reaches for the stars through dedication and purpose.

Reflection Questions:

- What past experiences shaped how you view stress?

- What do your triggers teach you about your mindset?

- What is your purpose?

- What is your identity?

CHAPTER 9

The Power of Cultivating Self-Love and Self-Respect

Now you've defined your purpose and a strong sense of who you are, stress feels lighter, and you can focus on what truly matters. When you know where you're going, you stop wasting your energy on distractions that don't serve you.

But here's the catch: this clarity only works if you respect yourself enough to protect it. If you allow external forces to pull you in different directions, drain your energy, or make you doubt your path, you lose your focus and grounding.

So, what's the real key?

Honoring your own boundaries and not allowing the outside world to shake what you've worked so hard to build on the inside.

Self-respect and self-love start with recognizing your worth and prioritizing your well-being. When you truly value yourself, you naturally set boundaries that protect your time, energy, and emotional health, and that, in turn, reduces stress.

By saying *no* to what doesn't serve you and *yes* to what aligns with your values and purpose, you cut down on feelings of guilt, resentment, and exhaustion, which are key contributors to chronic stress.

Loving yourself means making choices that support your well-being. Boundaries are the safeguards that ensure that your energy is spent on what uplifts you, not what rather depletes you.

Let me tell you this story.

During my first session with a coach back in 2019, I spent most of the hour venting about a frustrating situation with a colleague. I went on and on about how unfair it was and how difficult he was to work with.

After listening patiently, the coach asked me one simple question:

"What are you doing about it?"

I didn't hesitate.

"Nothing," I replied. "I can't do anything. He'll never change, and I can't fire him."

I listed all the things that were beyond my control and explained why I felt stuck.

She looked at me gently and said,

"Be kind to yourself. Love yourself."

At first, I was confused and even offended. *What did that have to do with anything?* Was she suggesting I didn't love myself? I brushed it off. But I didn't forget it.

It wasn't until three years later, after deep self-work and inner exploration, that her words finally made sense. Blaming others, avoiding boundaries, refusing to protect myself. These were all signs that I wasn't respecting myself. That lack of self-respect resulted in a lack of boundaries. It was the root cause of my stress, exhaustion, and overwhelm.

I would never say no to my boss or a subordinate. I saw myself as a "diplomat," always negotiating and finding a middle ground. But in the end, I took on the task, anyway.

Sounds familiar?

As a leader, I felt the constant need to be there for others and prove I was capable, reliable, and dedicated. I took on far more than I could handle—often doing the work of others.

I justified it by saying it came from a place of love, support, and dedication. And because this pattern showed up more often in my professional life than in my personal life, my brain found a clever way to lie to me: "You're not a people-pleaser; you're just a supportive leader."

But let me be clear: there's no real difference. Whether it's at home or at work, overextending yourself stems from the same root issue: a lack of boundaries.

And here's the tricky part: when you give endlessly, you unconsciously expect others to do the same. You assume they'll support you, help you, and be as available as you are. So, when they say *no,* you feel disappointed, shocked, even betrayed. You start building stories in your mind:

They're not supportive.

They don't care.

They don't show up like I do.

But the truth?

They're simply setting boundaries where you aren't.

I remember once during summer vacation, I sent my supervisor an urgent request via text. His response? "Sorry, I'm out with my kids and won't be able to respond for the next two days."

I was shocked. At first, I took it personally. At the time, I couldn't understand that his response wasn't about me. It was about him honoring his priorities. Instead, it triggered all my old patterns: guilt, over-responsibility, and the belief that a great leader is always available. That was in 2011, and I promised myself: "I'll never be the kind of leader who's unavailable to their team."

How wrong I was.

The Boundary Breakthrough

Everything clicked when I finally understood what boundaries really are. It wasn't about others crossing my limits; it was that I had never *set* them in the first place. I had no one to blame but myself.

Authors Dr. Henry Cloud and Dr. John Townsend say it best: boundaries are essential for emotional well-being, preventing burnout, and reducing stress.

Their research shows that chronic stress rarely comes from doing too much. It comes from not being able to say no.

Boundaries act as filters. They allow you to engage in what serves you and keep out what drains you, protecting your time, energy, and mental space from unnecessary stressors. Without them, you become overwhelmed, resentful, and emotionally depleted. You experience decreased productivity and strained relationships. By learning to set and communicate boundaries, you take back control of your time and energy. You prioritize your well-being and foster healthier, more balanced interactions. You teach others how to treat you. And you create space for what really matters.

Boundaries are not walls. They are invitations to healthier, more respectful relationships with others *and* yourself. People might still try to push them, but the difference is that *you* now know what you will and won't accept. That clarity is your power.

Beyond Work-Life Balance

For a long time, I thought setting boundaries meant fixing my working hours, turning off my laptop at 6 p.m., saying no to extra tasks, or not checking email on weekends. I thought it was about separating my work and personal life. But I was wrong.

I've learned that real boundaries aren't about rigid schedules or strict rules. They're about understanding what you need to stay well across *all* areas of life, including work, relationships, social time, and, most importantly, your inner world. Work and life aren't two separate compartments. They're all part of the same ecosystem: you.

Setting boundaries means defining what you allow in and what you protect. It's about navigating all parts of your life without losing yourself in the process.

So, let's talk about the boundary that matters most: the one you set within yourself.

Because if you don't prioritize self-respect, how can you expect others to respect you?

Boundaries start with you.

They begin with how you talk to yourself, how you manage your time, how you honor your energy, and how you make decisions.

When you choose self-respect, boundaries become easier. And when you commit to those boundaries, stress no longer runs your life. *You* do.

Ask yourself: "What am I no longer willing to accept from myself?" Is it:

- negative self-talk?

- constantly replaying the same unhelpful thoughts?

- breaking promises to yourself over and over again?

Once you identify these personal boundaries, think about what needs to be in place to uphold them. Don't overcomplicate it. Don't make it overwhelming. Start small. Self-respect isn't about drastic changes. It begins with simple actions, like:

- getting better sleep

- taking time for yourself

- doing something that genuinely nurtures you

For me, this was the hardest boundary to define, because at first, I didn't even realize I needed it. But over time, I began to notice all the little ways I wasn't respecting myself:

- telling myself, *Tomorrow, I'll go to the gym*, then skipping it because I was "too busy"

- planning to change my hair color, then deciding it wasn't necessary because I should use that time for my kids

- committing to reading 10 pages a day, only to scroll social media for two hours before bed, leaving me exhausted and drained

I made things easier. I started with just one boundary: I go to sleep whenever I feel sleepy (which annoys all my family members). And once I respected that single boundary, others followed naturally—without guilt, allowing myself to prioritize my needs in a way that felt natural and sustainable.

Because self-respect starts with the little things.

Once you begin setting boundaries in the five key areas—in your work, with your partner, in your social environment, with your family, and within yourself—ensure they align with your purpose and identity. There's no point in setting unrealistic or rigid boundaries that don't fit your life.

I remember a doctor I worked with who couldn't follow the "classic boundary" of not answering calls after 5 p.m. because some of her patients had serious conditions. That's exactly why boundaries aren't one-size-fits-all. What feels right and healthy for one person might not work for someone else, and that's okay.

Instead of forcing a rule that didn't fit her life, she redefined her boundaries.

She started delegating certain patients to colleagues on select days, shifted her cutoff time to 7 p.m., and protected specific weekends. That way, she remained available without sacrificing her well-being.

Boundaries aren't rules. They're a rhythm, a way of creating balance *your* way. But they need to be communicated.

You can't expect others to know your boundaries automatically. Everyone is different. Some may find your boundaries surprising, offensive, or even triggering. Others might resist them.

Be patient. Start small. As you grow more confident in expressing your needs, you'll reach a point where your boundaries are understood and respected without question.

When that happens, you'll experience the true freedom that comes from reduced stress, greater emotional clarity, and healthier relationship

Finding Balance Between Work and Personal Life

We often talk about "work-life balance," but let me challenge that: balance doesn't exist, or rather not in the way we think. What truly matters is harmony, a natural, fluid alignment across all the parts of your life: your work, social connections, relationships, family, and, most importantly, yourself.

Boundaries help create that harmony. They protect your energy and allow you to show up fully in each area. When your boundaries align with your purpose and identity, everything should finally click into place.

But does it?

Not always.

Sometimes, even when we set boundaries and define priorities, our minds don't cooperate. You might be at dinner with your family but thinking about emails. Or at work, feeling guilty about not being home.

This mental split is what I call the gray zone, that exhausting space where your body is in one place, but your mind is elsewhere.

You're playing with your kids, but your mind is racing with work emails.

You're at work but feel guilty for not spending more time with your partner.

You're never fully here, and your energy is constantly divided.

Dr. Jon Kabat-Zinn, a pioneer in mindfulness, explains that this constant mental tug-of-war is a major source of stress. It keeps us from being present in the moment.

How do you step out of the gray zone?

Here are two simple techniques I use to reclaim my energy and presence:

The Transition Ritual

Before switching from one role to another—work to home, home to work—pause for two minutes to reset. Do the following:

- Close your eyes.

- Take a deep breath.

- Mentally, tell yourself, "Now, I am stepping into this moment."

This tiny ritual signals your brain: We've shifted. Be here now. It makes it easier to release lingering thoughts from the earlier part of your day.

The Present Moment Anchor

When your mind drifts, don't judge. Just notice it like a neutral observer, and gently bring yourself back using your senses:

- What do I see? (Notice colors, objects, or people around you.)

- What do I hear? (Listen to voices, background sounds, or even silence.)

- What do I feel? (The chair under you, your breath, the warmth of your hands.)

These micro-moments of awareness anchor you in the now and pull you out of mental autopilot.

Setting boundaries isn't about putting up walls; it's about creating a life that supports your energy, your purpose, and your well-being. It's not selfish. It's self-respect. And when you begin with that, everything else starts to align.

Reflection Questions:

- Where in your life do you notice yourself slipping into the gray zone?

- What's one slight shift you can make today to create more harmony?

- What boundaries do you need to establish in your life?

- How can you honor your commitments to yourself more consistently?

CHAPTER 10

Practical Strategies to Conserve and Renew Your Mental, Emotional, and Physical Energy

Now that you've defined your purpose and identity, and you've protected your energy by setting clear boundaries, you've built a strong foundation. To go further, you need fuel to keep going. Just like a fire needs wood to keep burning, you need energy to sustain your momentum. Without it, even the most meaningful goals can feel exhausting. Let's talk about how to refuel yourself and stay committed, motivated, and resilient on your journey.

Reduce Overthinking

There was a time when my mind never stopped. It wasn't just busy; it was exhausting. From the moment I woke up to the second I fell asleep, my thoughts were in overdrive, replaying past conversations, planning every little detail, and worrying about things completely out of my control. It felt like I was carrying an endless to-do list in my head with no pause button.

I should have responded this instead of that.
Tomorrow, I will tell him I don't have time for that.
I need to cook five meals before I go on the business trip.

They need new shoes.

I forgot to pay the car insurance.

Did the project team book the photographer for the event?

Did the donor say YES to the new project?

I need to lose weight; I look awful.

Why is she taking all of July off while I'm working? I also have kids. She's so selfish.

This is just a glimpse of what used to run through my mind. On repeat. My brain was a constant, noisy battlefield every hour and every minute.

For years, I mistook being intelligent and successful for being an *overthinker*. I thought that planning everything made me productive. Sometimes, even at night, I was writing emails in my head instead of sleeping. I justified it by saying, *This is what high achievers do.* I had plans A and B for everything.

What didn't I realize? Overthinking was *exhausting* me.

I was constantly depleted, physically tired, but my brain refused to stop. And when you're exhausted, you can't perform at your best. You make mistakes, lose focus, start resenting others... and the spiral continues. It's a vicious cycle.

I had the illusion that I was solving problems, but the truth? I was stuck in a mental loop. Overthinking.

Overthinking, also called rumination, isn't harmless. Research shows it's strongly linked to fatigue, headaches, difficulty concentrating, and even prolonged stress responses in the body.

It's like running a marathon in your mind while standing completely still—exhausting, unproductive, and ultimately depleting.

You have roughly 60,000 thoughts per day. Studies show that 95% are repetitive, and 80% of those are negative. No wonder you feel drained!

The good news is that you can turn things around. If you're stuck in a mental spiral, know that you're not alone, and more importantly, you can break free.

Here are the two steps that helped me shift out of overthinking and into clarity.

Step 1: Notice It

Catching yourself in the act of overthinking is a game-changer. I used to spend hours overthinking without even realizing it, but awareness helped me break the loop.

Step 2: Interrupt the Spiral

Train yourself to get out of that state faster. That's what I did. It's not perfect, but it's *better*. My mind is quieter (relatively), my energy is higher, and most importantly I actually *solve* problems instead of obsessing over them.

Here's one additional technique I use that might help you, too. I call it the *Thought Triage Exercise.*

When I'm ruminating, I write every thought down. Then I ask:

Will I take action on this? → If yes, I assign a date to it.

Will I delegate this? → If yes, to whom and when?

Is this outside my control? → If yes, I let it go.

Letting go isn't easy.

But here's my trick: I visualize the thought as an object. I place it on a cloud and watch it drift away. Or I imagine it as a leaf floating down a river, carried away by the current.

It's a discipline, a practice to free your mind from unnecessary clutter and fill it with what truly matters.

Am I perfect at this? No.

But when I notice I'm spiraling, I literally say to myself:

Okay, Donya, you've been stuck on this for a while. What's the plan? Either do something about it, delegate it, or let it go.

Remember, overthinking drains your energy. And if you're not regularly refilling your cup, you'll end up running on empty.

So, catch it. Question it. Decide what to do with it. And then free yourself.

Holistic Energy Restore

I used to think taking a break would fix my exhaustion.

Just sleep more. Take a vacation. Unplug.

I did all of that. One summer, I went to Switzerland with my husband and three kids for ten days. I relaxed. I slept. I laughed. I disconnected. It was amazing. But the moment I came back?

Reality hit like a truck.

Within 24 hours, I felt just as overwhelmed as before. My mind picked up right where it left off, overanalyzing everything, worrying about what I'd missed, and stressing about what needed to be done. It was as if the vacation had never happened.

That's when I realized I wasn't refilling my energy cup. I wasn't truly *recharging*. I was just *pausing the stress.*

But energy isn't just about sleep or relaxation. It's about how you refuel yourself on all levels: physical, emotional, mental, and spiritual. When you neglect that, no amount of vacation time will truly restore you.

Energy isn't just physical; it's holistic.

Through trial and error (and many failed attempts at "fixing" exhaustion), I discovered that my energy is like a battery with four compartments. And if I only recharge one, I still feel depleted.

Here they are:

1. Physical energy

Sleep, nutrition, hydration, movement. We all know this. But rest alone can't fix a tired soul or an anxious mind.

2. Intellectual energy

Ever wake up rested but feel mentally foggy? Your brain needs more than rest; it needs stimulation. Reading, learning, and curiosity revive your mind. These activities also reduce overthinking.

3. Emotional energy

This comes from *connection*. A hug. A shared laugh. A moment of genuine presence with someone you care about. That fills your heart in ways rest never could.

4. Spiritual energy

This is about finding meaning and inner peace. For me, it's journaling, prayer, mindfulness, and time in nature. When I ignore this, even when everything else is "fine," I feel off-balance.

If you feel exhausted all the time, even when you rest, maybe you're not recharging all four compartments. You might get plenty of sleep yet starve for emotional or spiritual connection. You might be relaxing but not feeling intellectually or creatively stimulated.

Real energy management isn't just about rest. It's about restoration. Refill your whole self, not just your schedule.

Reflection Questions:

- What thoughts drain your energy, and how can you reframe them?

- What specific strategies can you use to refill each type of energy?

- How can you align your actions with what truly matters to you?

SECTION 4

THE ART OF EFFECTIVE NETWORKING
By Joël Vuadens-Chan

CHAPTER 11

Networking, A Key Skill for Your Career

You walk into a room full of strangers at a networking event. You're wearing your best clothes, carrying your brand-new business cards, and have even tailored a killer elevator pitch perfect for this occasion. But how do you find the right people, build meaningful connections, and stand out in a way that feels both authentic and strategic?

To help you fast-track the skills you need, I'll share the same tools I teach in my mentoring programs, the same tools that help professionals master their networking strategy with confidence. You'll learn how to identify the right events to attend, engage with the people who matter most to your goals, and position yourself as one of the most sought-after individuals in any room.

So that sounds like fun, right? At one point in my career, as a sales director and member of the executive board, my job involved attending cocktails and dinners with CEOs two to three times a week and getting paid to do it.

I wasn't great at networking in the beginning. But I had an advantage: I had frequent opportunities to practice. If something didn't go well, I knew I could try again two or three days later. Over time, two years, to be exact, I started to get the hang of it. That was over seven years ago. Since then, I've kept sharpening my networking skills.

I've attended Davos week during the World Economic Forum seven times, taken part in seven leadership training conferences, and continue to show up at a variety of high-level events. I knew only one or two people at most of these places when I first started out. But years later, I now get recognized, welcomed, and even invited into exclusive partnerships. People know who I am and what I bring to the table.

Now, let's get practical.

Before diving into tactics, we'll begin with a series of simple but powerful questions to help you shape a networking strategy that aligns with both your meeting type and your personality.

Here's the first one:

Why do you want to network? What's your reason?

Is it just about meeting more people? That's a great start, but what makes it meaningful to you? Why does it matter? Is it purely social, or are you hoping to grow your connections, find a new job, unlock opportunities, attract clients, or learn something new?

Take a moment to reflect and write down your answer.

Now, here's a slightly more challenging question:

Who would you like to meet?

If you don't have a specific name in mind, that's perfectly fine.

What matters is having clarity on the kind of person—or profile—you're hoping to connect with.

Are you looking to meet decision-makers in your industry? Creatives who inspire you? Potential clients, collaborators, or mentors? Think about the roles they play, the values they hold, or the influence they might have on your goals.

The clearer you are about who you're looking for, the easier it becomes to spot them in a crowd and, more importantly, to approach them with purpose and confidence.

Take a moment now to jot down a few ideas: titles, industries, qualities, or even just a vibe.

Make Your Entrance: Strategic Prep for Standout Networking

Let's start with something simple: the first step in successful networking is preparation.

But how do you actually prepare?

The first step is to find out who will be there.

Start with the easy part: research the speakers. Most conferences and events publish their speaker lineup weeks in advance. Look them up. What do they talk about? What industry are they in? Is there someone you'd love to connect with?

Getting information about the participants is a bit trickier when the attendee lists aren't public, but if you're a sponsor, or connected to one, you may have access.

However, many events now use dedicated platforms where participants can register, view the attendee list, and even interact before the event. Some even offer options to schedule short one-on-one meetings, often called "speed dates," with other attendees during the event.

Once you've got a few names, it's time to do your homework.

So, here's the next question:

If you want to know about somebody, where do you look?

Start with the basics:

- *LinkedIn*: This is your go-to. You can learn about someone's professional background, current role, shared connections, and even the topics they care about.

- *Company websites*: They are especially useful when it comes to speakers or executives. Look for bios, recent news, or projects they've led.

- *Social media*: Twitter (now X), Instagram, or even TikTok can give you a sense of their personality, interests, and thought leadership.

- *Podcasts, blogs, or YouTube channels*: If they're a content creator or have been interviewed, this is a goldmine for understanding their tone, values, and expertise.

- *Google search*: A simple search can go a long way. Look for any articles they've written, interviews they've given, or events where they've spoken. This can reveal their expertise, passions, and recent accomplishments, and it can give you great conversation starters.

Once you've researched people, you can create priority lists of those you'd like to meet.

Before attending an event, I usually identify 10 people I want to connect with. I can't be 100% sure they'll show up, unless they're speakers, but they're high on my list.

Here's a tip: if you're like me and struggle to remember faces you haven't met yet, look at their LinkedIn picture a few minutes before the event and try to remember them.

Also, bring a pair of glasses because name tags can be tiny.

So, now you're prepared. You've got your list of ten people, you've read up on them, you know what they look like, and you have a plan to recognize them when you get there.

Stick with me, because now we're getting very practical. Let's talk about being in the *right* spot during the event.

Strategic Positioning at Events

On the day itself, what should you do first? I'm going to shock you: arrive early! Very early! First, arriving early helps you feel relaxed and focused. Second, it gives you a head start. When you're among the first to show up, you get to own the room. You can start conversations before the crowd pours in, making meaningful connections before things get hectic.

At the last big conference I attended in London, I got there before the registration desk even opened. There were only about six or seven people waiting, and guess what happened? I spoke to all of them. By the time the crowd arrived, I had already connected with key participants. I was there first. I was ready. I had positioned myself for success.

That early arrival gives you another advantage: a strategic spot in the room. If you show up late, you're likely to end up at the back or tucked away in a corner, which is not ideal if you want to connect with people or be visible. If you want to interact with the speakers, choose a seat in the first or second row.

What's the best spot at an event? To find out, think beyond just your seat.

During the breaks—coffee, breakfast, networking sessions—positioning matters. For example, many events offer optional breakfasts before the first session. I always go. It's a perfect opportunity to meet people before the day kicks off.

Where should you stand or sit to meet and see people?

- *Near the aisle in front.* This gives you easier access to speakers and key attendees.

- *Center of the room.* You'll be more visible to others.

At the extended forum during WEF week in Davos, I attended small sessions with just 20 people, including top CEOs as speakers of panelists. I always sat in the first or second row. As soon as the talk ended, I'd jump up and start a conversation. I was only *five seconds* away from them, literally.

Ultimately, the final choice boils down to who you want to meet, how the room is set up, and how you can navigate your way to them. But remember, strategic positioning applies to different moments throughout the event.

Even waiting in line is a golden opportunity to make new, meaningful connections. Some of the best conversations happen when you're getting a coffee before the first session. Everyone's waiting. No one's in a rush.

People are open. Start talking. You've already got something in common: you're at the same event.

Don't hesitate to take advantage of:

- registration lines

- coffee lines

- waiting to talk to someone

Wherever there's a line, there's potential for connection. Let me give you an example.

I was once on a business trip in a quiet town in northern France. On the first evening, the only open place was a tiny pizza pickup joint. I had to wait 40 minutes. But by the time I got my order, I knew everyone in the room. There weren't many, but I had conversations with all of them.

The next day, I went to a small restaurant where only a few tables were occupied. One was taken by a local family whose son was studying at the university and preparing to go on an exchange. At another table sat a British couple, just passing through. I chatted with them while I waited for my food.

The following morning, I went down to breakfast at the small B&B where I was staying. It had only three rooms, so just three tables. There they were again, the same British couple. At the next table sat someone from the organization I was working with, someone I had only known by name. Before long, we were chatting as if we had a long history together.

The B&B owner looked at me and said, "Wow, you know everybody here."

She was right. That's what I mean by owning the place: being present and connecting with the people around you.

That small town in France was about 500 miles from my home. I had been there only once or twice. But I made a point of reaching out to everyone I could.

Why do I do that?

First, it is fun.

Second, it sharpens my people skills.

And third, people are genuinely grateful when you take the first step.

Now back to you and your networking event. You've found your place in the room and made contact. But how do you move beyond small talk? I've got you covered. In the next chapter, we'll explore how to go from great positioning to great conversations. From those conversations, you can build real partnerships and eventually achieve the results you're looking for.

Key Takeaways:

- Finding the right contacts in an event is a challenge. When you face a crowd, you first need to find out how you would like to meet them, then prepare yourself to meet them. Create a list of potential attendees.

- By showing up early, you position yourself in a strategic place to access them. If you do it right, you might even become the most popular person in the room.

CHAPTER 12

Breaking the Ice: How to Start Conversations That Build Connections

Now that you are in the room and in the right place, what's next? You start connecting with people. You spark conversations that lead to partnerships.

Isn't that what you were seeking through networking? I hope the answer is yes.

How do you start a conversation?

Here's where I might surprise you. I'm not a fan of elevator pitches. Why? Because they're self-centered. You talk only about yourself without knowing if your pitch is even relevant to the person in front of you. So instead of talking about yourself, ask an interesting question and listen. Give your undivided attention, expecting nothing in return. Sure, you want that contact link or opportunity, but put that aside for a moment. If you focus on building enough genuine relationships, you'll find your way to the right people, and the right doors will open.

Networking is not about you. It's about the people you're connecting with.

I have to remind myself of this constantly. Coming from a sales background, I tend to go straight to the goal. That transactional mindset? It's a close cousin of arrogance.

Now imagine everyone you meet delivers a perfect, polished introduction. It's all boilerplate. One after another:

"My company did this."

"I achieved that."

"I have these credentials."

By the fifth person, you're exhausted.

Instead, try this: "How are you doing today?" Or better: "How are you feeling?" "What do you think of the conference so far?" "How do you like this event?" "How is your day?"

It's already a perfect place to start. These simple questions break the mold. They create space for real connection. And that's the perfect place to start.

What If You're an Introvert?

Introverts are often the best networkers. They listen more than they speak. They ask thoughtful questions, take a genuine interest in others, and speak only when it truly adds value. That's the key: ask good questions.

Professor Nicholas Epley of the University of Chicago Booth School of Business, along with Juliana Schroeder, conducted a study titled "Mistakenly Seeking Solitude." The study explored the benefits of social interaction with strangers during commutes.

In the experiment, students were asked to strike up a conversation during their train ride. Beforehand, they completed a survey. One of the questions was: "How would you feel if you talked to a stranger?"

The most common fears?

"I'll look stupid."

"I'll make the other person uncomfortable."

Maybe you can relate, especially in a quiet setting where no one else is talking.

Professor Epley also took the challenge. On his next commute, he turned to a woman and said, "Oh, you have a beautiful hat." That simple compliment sparked a 20-minute conversation about life, family, and everything in between.

On a side note, I've tried this around the world, and it works. And it doesn't matter how you start.

"What's your name?" works. It is a good one. Another excellent question would be: "What challenges are you seeing in the market today?"

Let's go back to Professor Epley and his students. After the experiment, the participants filled out a follow-up survey. Every single one of them reported that the conversation went well and was genuinely appreciated. Professor Epley continued these connection experiments on his daily commute. Not once did anyone ignore him or reject the conversation.

The takeaway? Commuters who engaged with strangers reported far more positive experiences than those who sat in silence.

And that was on a train. Just imagine how much more welcome those conversations are at a business event where everyone expects to connect.

Give Without Expecting Anything in Return

Why did the experiment work so well?

The answer is simple: because they all start by asking questions instead of pushing their agenda, boasting, or trying to sell something. The questions could be broad or simple, anything that helps the other person feel seen and valued. Remember the top CEOs I tried to speak with in Davos during the World Economic Forum?

Instead of launching into who I was, I took notes during their speeches or panel discussions. Then, when I spoke to them, I referred to something they said that resonated with me and asked a thoughtful follow-up question. I was the only one doing that. Everyone else jumped straight into introductions and handing over their business cards.

I was networking at the *Bloomberg Technology Summit: Solving Global Challenges* on cybersecurity and AI in London in 2023 when I struck up a conversation with a small group that looked relatively young. As it turned out, they were students. I shifted gears and asked questions like: "What are you studying?" "Which topic do you prefer?" "What are you struggling with?" That small moment turned into an impromptu mentoring session—centered around a topic they were truly passionate about.

Here's the truth: people love talking about themselves, and so do you. But start with them. Talk *about* them. And as the conversation unfolds, stay curious. Ask follow-up questions. Find out more. From a sales perspective, this is a form of lead qualification.

You might ask:

- What kind of business are you in?

- What do you do for work?

And from there, you begin to understand: Is this someone who's a potential client, collaborator, or decision-maker? All of this helps you lead the conversation—and understand if there's a genuine match for what you're about.

If you're job hunting, ask yourself:

- Is this person a decision-maker?

- Could they recommend you?

- Are they just starting out, maybe an intern?

It makes a big difference.

And here's something powerful: when you ask thoughtful questions, other people are drawn in. You might suddenly find yourself hosting a mini-discussion. That's why people attend events in the first place: to connect. Ask one good question to a small group, and you create space for others to open up and learn from each other. That's real networking.

One of the most powerful networking principles is simple: add value expecting nothing in return. That alone makes you magnetic. They want to talk to someone who's genuinely curious, kind, and present—someone who's there to serve, not to take. This kind of presence is rare. So don't be surprised if you end up being seen as the most popular and the most generous person in the room. And the world needs more of that.

Does it feel good for the other person? Of course it does. Does it feel good to you? Absolutely.

Not everybody needs to hear your life story or your business pitch, especially if they're not the right fit. But everybody needs to be cared for. It's empathy. It's compassion.

Leadership expert John C. Maxwell titled one of his books, *Everyone Communicates, Few Connect*. This is so true. Most people broadcast. Few truly network in the way we're talking about here. In another one of his books, *The 21 Irrefutable Laws of Leadership*, Law #10 says:

"Leaders touch a heart before they ask for a hand." This principle highlights the power of emotional connection as the foundation for effective leadership and inspiration.

At home, my wife decorated our office. The wall behind my desk looks like a virtual background, but it is not. She placed inspiring quotes, including one of my favorites: "In a world where you can be anything: Be kind." It sits right behind me, a daily reminder to lead with kindness. During conference calls, I'll often reach back, pick up the framed quote, and show it on camera. It creates a moment of reflection for both me and the person I'm speaking with.

The truth is, we don't know what people are going through. We don't know their challenges. But we can give them space to feel safe. We can connect through empathy and compassion. That's what leads to trust. That's what builds genuine relationships. Because networking isn't about you. It's about the other person.

The Art of Connecting People

Do you think you don't know anybody in the room? Start by speaking to five or six people. Chances are that the seventh person you meet has a challenge that one of the first six can help solve.

That's your golden moment.

You say, "I just met somebody in that field. Can I introduce you to that person?" Just like that, you've gone from a networker to a connector in a room full of strangers. How powerful is that?

So yes, it's all about connection!

But what if you walk into a room where everyone *already* seems to know each other?

People are clustered in tight little groups. You're alone. It feels intimidating. What do you do?

Most of us have faced this before and will again. I've certainly been there many times. Here's one approach that works wonders: find just one person. Befriend them early on. They become your anchor. It's not about whether you know them. It's about whether they know you.

Now, let's say your new connection drifts over to another group. You follow at a respectful distance. When they join a circle of people, you do something simple but powerful: you stand just outside the circle. Wait a minute or two. Then, like magic, something will happen, because most people are polite and welcoming. The circle will open, and you'll be invited in. Even better, your new friend will probably introduce you to the others. And just like that, you're in.

When you join, first listen. Give it a few minutes. Then, offer a sincere compliment or a thoughtful question. Don't force your introduction; let the moment come. Someone will eventually turn to you and ask, "And what do you do?" That's your moment. Introduce yourself but keep it short.

Some circles are hard or nearly impossible to break, especially when executives are surrounded by "visual bodyguards" and a wall of closed-off energy. Yet often, all it takes is one person to change that dynamic. Be patient. Don't push it. Stay open, and you'll find the right opportunity. And remember, the best conversations often happen when and where you least expect them.

Introducing others is one of the most generous, effective ways to build trust and raise your reputation at any event. I used this approach at an international cooperation conference where I was hoping to meet a university professor. A friend of mine also wanted an introduction, so I made sure to introduce her first. By doing that, I added value to both parties and helped my friend make a meaningful connection, all while naturally transitioning into the conversation I had been hoping to have myself.

Offer Partnerships Effectively

Most people lead with this, but they shouldn't. You've seen it before: someone meets you and within seconds they're handing you a book, a link, a QR code, or launching into a pitch. Am I exaggerating? Maybe just a little.

Yes, I attend events to find partners, clients, or opportunities. But I don't mention any of that at the start. I wait until I've qualified the contact.

In sales, qualification means determining whether someone is a viable prospect. In networking, it's the same idea. Once I know it's the right person, then and only then do I explore the possibility of a partnership.

If they mention they're looking for coaching, leadership development, or team building, I ask pointed questions about how the teams are doing regarding the company culture. If I sense they're a decision-maker and facing challenges, I might say: "You mentioned some struggles in your team. I have a few ideas that might help. Would you be open to continuing this conversation?"

But I never single them out in front of a group. I save that invitation for later, often mentioning it in a follow-up message.

The Future of Networking: Digital Business Cards Done Right

Now that you've built a connection, how do you capture information from potential partners or collaborators? Ask for their business card. Yes, they still exist!

I also connect via LinkedIn using the QR code feature, but I always ask for their card. Why? Because the card they give me holds more value than the one I give out. When I receive a card, I write key details on the back, such as something memorable they said or a challenge they shared. For example: *toxic company culture.*

Why? Because after an event, I might end up with fifty or more cards and quickly forget who said what. A quick note will help me recall the conversation and reconnect more meaningfully later. I also snap a photo of myself with the person, when possible.

Then, in my follow-up email, I might say:

"It was great meeting you. I enjoyed our chat about the challenges you're facing with your company's culture. Would you like to schedule a time to explore some ideas?"

Their own words become the bridge to continue the conversation. I can even attach the photo I took, so they remember the "nice person they met at the event."

Digital business card apps like *HiHello* or *Blinq* are also useful for keeping contacts organized and accessible.

Remember, you are not one thing. Neither are they. You might wear several hats—working with companies, universities, governments—and your message should adapt based on who you're speaking with. So should your business cards. Therefore, consider having more than one.

For example, I'm involved with universities, companies, and governments, and my value proposition varies depending on who I'm speaking to. That's why a one-size-fits-all elevator pitch doesn't work for me.

When I meet someone new, I don't jump into a boilerplate introduction. Instead, I ask questions first. That way, I can tailor what I share to what's most relevant and valuable to *them*. It's not just more effective; it makes the conversation more engaging for both of us.

If I meet someone in IT, I might say, "I'm an engineer too, but a people engineer. I help organizations design better team dynamics so they can innovate and collaborate more effectively."

People often respond with: "Wow, it would be nice to work together."

Sometimes, the person I meet already works with the company I'd like to reach. And we end up exploring how we might partner on future opportunities. That's why I take notes. Every conversation is unique.

People often decide about *you* before they decide what they want to do *with* you. It's common for someone to say, "I really enjoyed our conversation. We should find a way to work together." What they're responding to is *you*: your presence, energy, and how you made them feel. The idea or partnership often comes later.

When Will and I first met, we simply enjoyed talking, realizing we have many things in common. Later, we realized there were many ways we could collaborate, including a podcast, a conference, and more. It developed naturally.

Often, partnerships don't start with a pitch. They begin with good conversation, just like dating. So, enjoy the conversation first. The rest will follow.

Networking Is Fun

Many people see networking as hard work and often find it disappointing. But it doesn't have to be. When you shift your mindset and view it as an opportunity for authentic connection and personal growth, networking becomes not just productive, but genuinely enjoyable.

Repeating the same pitch over and over is dull. But discovering someone's passions, challenges, and dreams? That's exciting.

The cherry on the cake comes from being able to help by offering your expertise or connecting them with someone else.

John Maxwell said it best: "Sometimes you win, sometimes you learn." In other words, even when things don't go as planned, you still gain something valuable: insight that helps you grow.

This is especially true in networking. The more you practice, the more confident and authentic you become. Over time, networking starts to feel natural and even fun. Most importantly, it becomes a meaningful way to add value to others. In networking, we might say: *Always you network, sometimes you partner.*

Practice the principles presented in this section of the book, and you'll begin to enjoy networking as you learn, grow, and create meaningful connections. At your next event, go in with curiosity and generosity.

Discover interesting people. Connect them. Help them. And maybe, just maybe, partner with them.

Good networking!

Key Takeaways:

- Networking isn't about you; it's about creating value for others.

- Approach every conversation with a mindset of helping. That attitude naturally opens doors and often leads you to the connections you're truly looking for.

SECTION 5

PUBLIC SPEAKING FOR SUCCESS
By Neha Deshpande

CHAPTER 13

Public Speaking: The Game Changer

Warren Buffett has famously remarked that public speaking is not just a skill, but a powerful asset that can enhance your career for a lifetime. He has emphasized that strong communication skills can dramatically boost your earning potential, making them one of the smartest investments you can make in yourself.

Early in my career, I believed that my technical expertise and business acumen would be enough to propel me forward. But as I climbed the corporate ladder, I encountered situations that required me to speak to large audiences beyond my immediate team. The first time I stood in front of a crowd, fear almost paralyzed me. Still, I understood the importance of rising to the occasion. I embraced the opportunity and committed to preparing thoroughly for my presentation.

Regrettably, it didn't go as I'd hoped. I stumbled, forgetting a key line and freezing in the moment. Though it lasted only seconds, it felt like an eternity. That setback taught me a valuable lesson: to become an impactful speaker, I had to intentionally develop and refine my public speaking skills.

In this section of the book, we will delve into essential topics such as effective preparation, crafting powerful messages, understanding your audience, and navigating various communication channels. These insights will serve as your roadmap to becoming a confident and interesting speaker, unlocking new opportunities and speeding up your career growth.

Power Prep for Your Big Speaking Moment

The very first step on your public speaking journey is to sharpen your skills. Consistent practice and deliberate refinement of your delivery are essential. Clear, confident communication can make all the difference in how your audience receives and engages with your content.

Equally important is having a relevant, compelling message. Your content should resonate with your audience's interests and needs, offering insights that hold their attention and deliver real value. When your message speaks directly to them, engagement naturally follows.

By focusing on these two pillars—mastering your delivery and shaping a powerful, meaningful message—you'll dramatically increase your impact and confidence as a public speaker.

Becoming the Speaker Everyone Remembers

Public speaking is an art, and the speaker is at its heart. The speaker remains one of the most crucial elements of any successful presentation. Too often, speakers get so engrossed in their visual aids and slides that they forget they themselves are the primary source of the message. While visual aids can certainly enhance a presentation, relying on them entirely is a mistake.

There are three key factors that shape the unique voice of any speaker:

- their motivation and passion while delivering their presentation

- their communication skills

- their unique style and personal growth in sharing insights and ideas

To become a charismatic public speaker, keep these essentials in mind:

1. Know the Purpose

Before you begin preparing, clarify the purpose of your speech. What is the core message you want to convey? Are you aiming to inspire, inform, persuade, or something else?

Defining your purpose will shape every step of your preparation.

2. Keep it Simple

Clarity is key. Simple, direct language makes it easier for your audience to follow along and absorb your message. The goal is to create connection, not confusion.

Avoid jargon and unnecessary complexity; instead, speak in a way that's easy to understand and engaging to hear.

3. Be Flexible

Don't cling rigidly to your script. If you sense your audience is drifting, be ready to pivot. Shift your tone, switch up your delivery, or insert a relevant story or question to recapture their attention. Great speakers read the room and adjust in real time.

4. Connect with Your Audience

Avoid sounding boastful or making your audience feel talked down to. Instead, aim to be authentic, approachable, and even humorous when appropriate. You may be the expert, but they're here to learn, not to feel left behind. Tailor your speech to their level of understanding and make the experience enjoyable and relatable.

5. Stay Updated

Current events and emerging trends can enrich your message and build credibility. Referencing timely topics shows your awareness and helps your audience connect your content to the real world. Stay informed by reading widely and following thought leaders in your field.

6. Practice Makes You Perfect

Public speaking is a skill, and like any skill, it gets better with practice. Whether you're speaking to a packed auditorium or just a small team, every opportunity sharpens your delivery, refines your tone, and enhances your ability to engage your audience. It also helps you to improve your timing and strengthen your confidence. The more you do it, the more natural it becomes.

7. Record Yourself

Reviewing recordings of your speeches is one of the most powerful ways to improve. You'll catch things you might miss in the moment, such as unclear messaging, filler words, pacing issues, awkward pauses, or distracting body language. Watching yourself helps you gain objectivity and track your progress over time.

Remember, the journey to becoming a charismatic public speaker is ongoing, but also deeply rewarding. Keep refining your skills, stay passionate, and enjoy every step of the process.

From Thought to Impact: Sharpening Your Core Message

A clear, well-defined message is the foundation of every successful speech. When your message is focused, it aligns every element of your delivery—both verbal and non-verbal—with your core objective. Before speaking, take time to reflect on your core message. What do you want your audience to walk away with? Is it a call to action, a lesson, or an emotional response? Defining this purpose upfront will shape your content and elevate your impact.

A powerful message gives your speech direction and keeps your speech cohesive. Without that clarity, your audience might struggle to follow or, worse, forget the key points entirely. The goal is to leave them with a message that resonates and inspires long after you've left the stage.

Every powerful message is built on three core components:

- Content

- Style

- Structure

Let's take a closer look at each one.

1. Content

Content is at the core of your presentation. It's what carries your message and keeps your audience engaged. To make it effective, start by understanding who you're speaking to and tailor your material to their interests, needs, and level of understanding.

Focus on the key points you want your audience to remember. Avoid overwhelming them with too much information. Instead, aim for clarity, conciseness, and impact. Use solid facts, relevant data, and real-life examples to support your message and boost credibility. Stories, in particular, help make your content relatable and memorable. Focus on the key points you want them to remember.

2. Style

Style refers to how you deliver the content of your speech. It can range from formal to conversational, depending on what best suits the audience and occasion. A well-chosen style can significantly elevate the impact of your message, making it more relatable, engaging, and memorable.

To master your style, you need a strong understanding of your audience and the context in which you're speaking. Who are they? What tone will resonate with them? Is the setting professional, intimate, or inspirational?

Being aware of different communication styles and their effects is key to becoming an effective speaker. Developing this adaptability will allow you to tailor your delivery with purpose and precision, ensuring your message lands with lasting impact.

3. Structure

The structure of your speech should act like a hammock that holds everything together and guides your audience from start to finish in a clear and engaging way. A well-structured speech—with a strong introduction, a compelling body, and a memorable conclusion—keeps your audience engaged and ensures your message is heard.

Your introduction should grab attention and set the tone. The body is where you lay out your main points or arguments with clarity and purpose. Finally, the conclusion should reinforce your message and leave a lasting impression. A logical flow between sections helps your audience follow along easily and prevents confusion. Without a sound structure, even your best ideas can get lost, and along with them, your audience's attention.

Here's another trick. All impactful talks and speeches have one thing in common: the speaker introduces the key message, often called the hook, early on.

You have a couple of options here: you can either state your key message directly at the very beginning or subtly hint at it, building curiosity before revealing it later as the solution. Both approaches are powerful tools for capturing your audience's attention and setting the stage for what's coming.

As you progress through your speech, ensure that each point you make ties back to the key message. This creates a clear, cohesive narrative and helps reinforce your central idea.

When it's time to conclude, return to your key message. Repeating it at the end solidifies its importance and ensures your audience walks away with a lasting impression of your main point. Think of it as bookending your speech: open strong with your message, build around it, and close by driving it home.

To help convey your message with clarity and impact, consider using the 7 C's model.

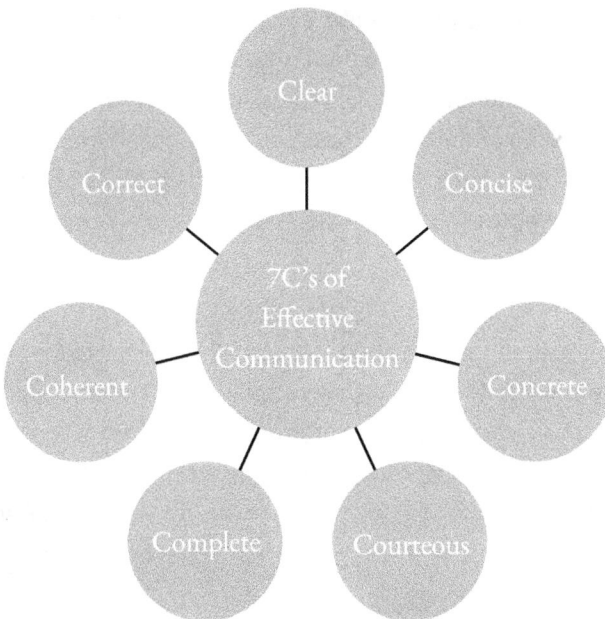

1. Clear

Clarity begins with simplicity. Use straightforward language and focus on the core points of your message to ensure it's easily understood by everyone. Avoiding idioms or jargon to prevent ambiguity, especially when speaking to diverse audiences who may not share the same cultural references.

Before you communicate, take time to clarify your own thoughts. Know exactly what you want to say and why you're saying it. When your message is clear in your own mind, it naturally becomes clearer to others.

2. Concise

Keep your sentences short and to the point. Clear, succinct communication is more likely to hold your audience's attention and prevent confusion. Eliminate unnecessary words while still conveying the full meaning of your message. Less is often more when it comes to effective speaking.

3. Concrete

Support your ideas with specific facts, data, or examples. Vague language weakens your message, while clear evidence strengthens your credibility and makes your points easier to understand.

Use precise modifiers; avoid general terms like "many" or "some." Instead, say "75% of the participants" or "three out of five respondents." Steer clear of broad generalizations or unverified opinions. Specificity adds power to your words.

4. Courteous

Speak with respect, warmth, and professionalism. A courteous tone builds rapport and creates a positive connection with your audience. Be open and honest in your message; transparency fosters trust. Even when addressing difficult topics, kindness and tact can ensure your communication is effective and well-received, which ultimately leads to better collaboration and outcomes.

5. Complete

A complete message includes all the information your audience needs to take the next step. One of the most powerful tools you can use is a strong call to action because it turns your message into something actionable. When you clearly state what you want the audience to do, you reduce ambiguity and make it easy for them to respond. Whether you're inviting your audience to attend a meeting, respond to a survey, or follow up on a task, the call to action directs them in the right direction. Enhance accessibility by including helpful links or resources, so they don't have to search for additional information. A complete message saves time, avoids confusion, and increases the chances of getting a response.

6. Coherent

Your message should make sense, flow logically, and stay consistent in tone and content.

Organize your ideas in a way that guides your audience naturally from one point to the next. This makes it easier to follow your message and reinforces understanding. Whether you're writing an email, giving a speech, or leading a meeting, consistency in style and structure helps maintain clarity and builds trust in your communication.

7. Correct

Accuracy is non-negotiable in effective communication. This includes using proper grammar and punctuation, ensuring facts are accurate, and double-checking names and job titles. Mistakes can undermine your professionalism and credibility. Always tailor your language to match your audience's level of understanding. Avoid jargon if it's unfamiliar to them and choose terms that match their knowledge and experience. Precision and correctness reflect respect, care, and a commitment to excellence.

Becoming a master of the 7 C's—Clear, Concise, Concrete, Courteous, Complete, Coherent, and Correct—will enable you to communicate with confidence, clarity, and impact. Whether you're delivering a speech, sending a message, or leading a conversation, applying these principles helps build stronger relationships, reduce misunderstandings, and inspire action. And remember that communication is a skill. Everyone makes mistakes now and then, and that's okay. The key is to recognize them and turn them into learning opportunities. The more you practice, the better you'll get—so keep refining, keep learning, and enjoy the process of becoming a truly effective communicator. By doing so, you'll build stronger connections and improve your interactions both at work and in your personal life.

Reflection Questions:

Here's a checklist to help you be an effective speaker and deliver a strong message:

1. Know Your Purpose

- Have you clearly defined the primary message or goal of your presentation?
- Is your message relevant to your audience?

2. Structure Your Presentation

- Does your speech have a clear introduction, body, and conclusion?
- Have you organized your ideas logically, ensuring a smooth flow?

3. Use the 7 Cs for an Effective Message

- Are you using simple and understandable language for your audience?
- Are you using the 7 Cs to convey your message effectively?

4. Incorporate Visual Aids

- Have you used visuals (slides, images, or videos) to support and clarify your message?
- Are your visuals clear, relevant, and not too distracting?

5. Practice Effective Delivery

- Are you practicing good vocal variety (tone, pitch, speed)?
- Are you using appropriate body language (gestures, eye contact, posture)?
- Do you speak with confidence and enthusiasm?

6. Summarize the Key Takeaways

- Have you summarized the main points at the end to reinforce your message?
- Have you included a call to action or something for your audience to think about?

Use this checklist to ensure you are fully prepared to deliver an impactful and effective presentation.

CHAPTER 14

Set the Stage

Communication is a dynamic process that involves three essential components: the source (the speaker or sender of the message), the channel (the medium through which the message is delivered, such as voice, visuals, or gestures), and the receiver (the audience or listener). This basic communication model is just as relevant in everyday conversations as it is in public speaking.

In a speech, the source is the person (speaker) delivering it, namely the individual who shares their ideas and engages with the audience. They must craft a clear message and deliver it effectively through spoken words, tone, visuals, and body language. This is the channel through which the message travels. The receiver comprises the audience members who interpret and react to the message, and their perspective plays a critical role in how the speech is received. Understanding your audience and adjusting your speech to resonate with them is key to delivering an effective and impactful presentation.

From Speaker to Listener: Building the Bridge

In public speaking, connecting with your audience is paramount, ensuring that they don't just hear your message, but truly internalize it. Stay attuned to their reactions and adjust as needed to maintain engagement. Personal anecdotes are a powerful way to build empathy and add emotional depth, making your message more relatable and memorable. Prioritize audience connection and empathy to elevate the impact of your public speaking and effectively promote your message.

An essential part of audience connection is respectful awareness. Avoid stereotyping—assuming that all members of a group share the same traits—and steer clear of totalizing, where one characteristic (such as a disability) is seen as the defining feature of a person. These missteps can damage relationships and diminish the impact of your message.

To speak effectively, conduct a thoughtful audience analysis before every presentation. Consider not only who your audience is, but how they might perceive you. Adapt your message, tone, and even your attire to align with their expectations and needs. This mindful preparation ensures your communication is not only effective, but ethical and inclusive.

When analyzing your audience, consider the following essential elements:

- their requirements

- their gender

- their race

- their location

- their profession or trade

- their activity

- the type of group (homogeneous or heterogeneous)

All the aspects we've discussed shape how you choose to present your material. Once you understand your audience, the next step is keeping them engaged throughout your speech or presentation.

Capturing and Keeping Attention

One of the most valuable lessons I learned in my public speaking journey was shifting from a "speaker-focused" approach to an "audience-focused" one. In today's fast-paced world, where digital devices and media are constantly vying for our attention, capturing and maintaining the audience's focus is more important than ever.

Attention is our most valuable resource. To communicate effectively, we must first earn it amidst distractions. But capturing attention is just the beginning. The real challenge is keeping it. That requires a powerful delivery and a message that's clear, relevant, and engaging, one that sparks connection and holds your audience from start to finish.

To truly connect with your audience and keep them engaged, try using these three proven strategies:

1. Start with a Strong Hook

Open with something that instantly grabs attention, such as a surprising fact, a provocative question, or a compelling story. A strong hook sets the tone and sparks curiosity, making your audience eager to hear what comes next.

2. Use Visual Aids

Incorporating images, videos, or infographics makes your message more visually engaging and easier to understand. Visuals can simplify complex ideas, break up long stretches of spoken content, and leave a lasting impression.

3. Encourage Interaction

Create opportunities for two-way communication. Whether it's asking questions, inviting feedback, or including moments for discussion, interaction builds involvement. It shows your audience that their input matters and makes your message more relevant and resonant.

But how do you gauge your audience's level of engagement?

Let's explore three key categories of audience engagement.

1. Physical Engagement

As the saying goes, "Where the body goes, the brain will follow." This emphasizes the power of involving your audience physically to boost interest and participation. Whether you're delivering an in-person presentation, leading a virtual meeting, or speaking to a group, incorporating physical actions can significantly increase engagement.

Examples include watching a video, reading a handout, clicking on interactive elements, raising hands, or using virtual reactions. Simple prompts like "turn to the person next to you and greet them" or "read the slide and share your thoughts" transform listeners into active participants. These physical activities create a dynamic atmosphere, more engaging and memorable.

2. Mental Engagement

Keeping your audience mentally engaged is essential to maintain their focus throughout your presentation. Here are three effective ways to do this: asking questions, sharing surprising facts or data, and using analogies.

First, asking questions throughout your presentation encourages the audience to think and interact, making them more engaged and attentive.

Second, presenting intriguing facts or bold statements sparks curiosity and makes your audience want to learn more. For example, saying something like, "30% of customer service issues could be solved with better training" grabs attention and invites deeper reflection.

Finally, analogies make complex ideas easier to understand by linking them to familiar concepts. Just be sure they are relatable because overly complicated or niche comparisons can confuse rather than clarify.

3. Linguistic Engagement

Linguistic engagement makes your communication more relatable and inclusive, encouraging your audience to connect deeply with your message.

Using inclusive language is key. People naturally respond to hearing their own names and the word "you." Incorporating phrases like "As you know..." or "You may be wondering..." into your speech creates a conversational tone that makes listeners feel personally involved. For example, you might say, "As you know, our team's success is built on collaboration," or "You may be wondering how we can improve our communication skills."

Time-traveling language takes your audience on a journey through past or future moments. Phrases like "Imagine..." or "What if you could..." will help them envision exciting possibilities ahead, making them feel enthused about what's to come. A good example would be, "Imagine how our productivity would soar if we all mastered these techniques." Conversely, phrases like "Remember when..." or "Think back to when..." will take your audience into the past, fostering a sense of reflection. A good example would be, "Think back to when we launched our first project and how far we've come since then."

Finally, connecting people through shared experiences or beliefs is a powerful way to create common ground. Highlighting your company's mission and values, or referencing past shared experiences, makes the message more relatable and fosters unity, much like friends or family reminiscing about good times. For example, saying, "Our commitment to innovation and excellence has always been at the heart of our success," or "Remember when we celebrated our last milestone together? That sense of achievement is something we can all relate to," can resonate with your audience and reinforce a sense of belonging.

By applying these techniques, you foster a sense of inclusion and engagement, creating deeper connections and a more unified, collaborative atmosphere for everyone involved.

Mastering Your Channel

The channel is the pathway through which a message travels from the sender (speaker) to the receiver (audience). As a speaker, you have access to various channels—spoken word, visuals, slides, video, written materials—and the most effective communicators choose their channels intentionally based on their audience and objective. Communication is the backbone of our collaboration and understanding how to leverage the different channels available to us can truly enhance our interactions.

1. Verbal Communication

This channel includes face-to-face conversations, phone calls, and video conferences. This channel is highly dynamic as it allows for immediate feedback and clarification. Elements like tone, pitch, and speed add emotional nuance and emphasis that written communication may lack. However, one challenge is that verbal exchanges can be hard to recall unless documented or followed up in writing.

To maximize the impact of verbal communication, consider the following best practices:

a. *Choose your words carefully*: Every word matters. Whether speaking or writing, aim for clarity and simplicity. Keep your sentences direct and avoid slang or filler words that might confuse your audience. Clear and concise communication ensures that your message is understood as intended.

b. *Listen actively*: Active listening is a cornerstone of effective communication. By showing genuine interest in the audience's questions, feedback, or concerns, you foster a deeper understanding and encourage collaboration. To practice active listening, eliminate distractions, focus fully on the speaker, and ask clarifying questions to ensure you've accurately received the information.

c. *Be yourself*: Authenticity goes a long way. Whether speaking to an individual or a group, avoid coming across as pretentious or arrogant. A humble, honest approach helps you build rapport and create a meaningful connection with your audience.

d. *Mind your tone:* The tone of your voice can significantly affect how your message is received. A natural, friendly, and respectful tone makes your communication more engaging and impactful. Remember, people often respond more to how you say something than to what you say.

2. Written Communication

This channel comprises emails, reports, and chat messages. The strength of this channel lies in its ability to provide a permanent record of our discussions, allowing for carefully crafted messages and ensuring everyone has access to the same information. On the other side, written communication can sometimes lack the immediacy and personal touch of verbal interactions.

To maximize the impact of written communication, consider the following best practices:

a. *State your goal clearly*: The primary goal of written communication is to present your message clearly and succinctly so that the reader can easily understand your point. Whether you're providing instructions, sharing information, or requesting action, be specific about what you want the reader to do or understand. Ambiguity can lead to confusion, so ensure you're direct and transparent. Clearly articulating the desired outcome prevents misunderstandings and ensures alignment with your message. This clarity enhances the overall effectiveness of your written communication.

b. *Keep it simple*: Avoid using jargon, complex vocabulary, or industry-specific expressions. Aim to make your messages accessible to everyone, regardless of their familiarity with your organization or field. This promotes inclusivity and ensures that no one feels confused or left out due to unclear language.

c. *Stay on the topic*: Stick to the core message and avoid irrelevant details. Clarity is key because concise communication helps readers stay focused and absorb your message more efficiently. Eliminate fluff and prioritize information that adds value and supports your main point.

3. Non-verbal Communication

This channel encompasses body language, facial expressions, and even the way we dress. These cues can significantly influence how our messages are perceived. For instance, a smile can indicate friendliness, while crossed arms might suggest defensiveness. Non-verbal communication often complements verbal communication, adding depth to our interactions. However, it can be easily misinterpreted without the context provided by verbal or written explanations. Often overlooked, non-verbal cues are incredibly impactful and can make a big difference in how effectively your message is received.

To maximize the impact of non-verbal communication, consider the following best practices:

a. *Make eye contact*: Eye contact is one of the most impactful nonverbal cues in communication. It helps keep your audience engaged, enhances your credibility, and builds a sense of connection. When you look people in the eye, they feel seen and involved.

b. *Use positive gestures*: Gestures play a significant role in emphasizing key points. Gestures can help channel your nerves into movement, provided they are not repetitive or distracting from your message.

c. *Leverage audience proximity*: Physical presence matters. Moving closer to your audience or offering a genuine smile can instantly build connection and warmth. Remember, your audience sees you before they hear you—use that moment to set a positive emotional tone and establish trust before a single word is spoken.

d. *Pay attention to facial expressions*: Your face speaks volumes—often before you say a word. Facial expressions reflect your feelings, thoughts, and intentions, making them a powerful tool in communication. A genuine smile can convey confidence, warmth, and friendliness, immediately putting others at ease. Conversely, a furrowed brow or tense expression might signal discomfort, doubt, or disapproval, unintentionally shifting the mood of the room. Be mindful of what your face is saying because it's often louder than your voice.

e. *Be mindful of posture*: Posture plays a critical role in first impressions. Many of us are unaware of how we carry ourselves, yet it communicates a great deal before we speak. Standing tall with your back straight, chin level, and eyes forward signals you're confident and prepared. Practicing power poses before speaking can help boost your presence and self-assurance.

f. *Use purposeful movement*: Movement is a visual cue that captures attention and reinforces your presence. When done intentionally, it signals confidence and command. Lean in slightly to show engagement or walk the stage to emphasize key points. Each step you take can create a sense of momentum and energy. Just be sure your movement is deliberate, not distracting. Done right, it enhances your credibility and strengthens your leadership presence.

g. *Incorporate vocal variety*: Your voice is a powerful tool for keeping attention. Infusing your speech with vocal variety—changes in pitch, pace, and tone—keeps your delivery energized and your audience engaged. A monotone voice can drain even the most brilliant message of its impact. Memorizing your speech word for word may seem safe, but it often leads to robotic delivery. Instead, focus on your key points and allow space for spontaneity. This not only adds authenticity but also builds a genuine connection with your listeners. Match your vocal delivery to the setting and message, whether it's raising your voice for emphasis or softening it to draw your audience in. The goal is to be heard *and* felt.

Interestingly, we often use more than one communication channel at once. Take a video conference, for example: we speak (verbal), share slides or documents (written), and respond to facial expressions and gestures (non-verbal), all simultaneously. When used strategically, this layering of channels can dramatically boost the clarity and impact of our message.

Being intentional about which channels we use and how allows us to tailor our communication to both the audience and the situation. By leveraging the unique strengths of each channel, we foster deeper understanding, enhance collaboration, and create a more dynamic presence. When these elements work in harmony, your message becomes not only clear, but compelling—one that resonates and inspires action.

Reflection Questions

Here's a checklist to help you consider your audience and use the appropriate channels effectively in public speaking:

1. Understand Your Audience

- Have you researched your audience's demographics, interests, expectations, and knowledge level?

- Are you aware of any affecting cultural or contextual factors that may affect your message?

2. Tailor Your Message

- Is your content relevant to the audience's needs and concerns?

- Have you adapted your language, tone, and examples to fit their preferences and level of understanding?

3. Select the Right Communication Channel

- Are you delivering your speech in the most suitable format (in-person, virtual, hybrid)?

- Have you selected the right tools (microphones, slides, video, etc.) to match the medium of delivery?

4. Create Engagement

- Have you planned ways to keep the audience engaged through questions, discussions, or activities?

- Are you ensuring the content is digestible and not overloaded with information?

5. Be Mindful of Audience Attention

- Have you structured your speech to maintain the audience's focus (clear introduction, smooth transitions, strong conclusion)?

- Are you using vocal variety, gestures, and eye contact to keep the audience engaged?

- Have you considered the length of your speech to avoid audience fatigue?

6. Channel Accessibility:

- Are your visuals, handouts, or any digital materials accessible and easy to understand?

- Have you accounted for audience accessibility needs (e.g., subtitles, sign language interpreters, screen readers)?

- Is your content inclusive, respectful, and free from biases?

This checklist helps you stay centered on your audience's needs while making the most of the right channels and tools to deliver your message with clarity, confidence, and impact.

CHAPTER 15

Make a Lasting Impact

Public speaking can be challenging, but with the right techniques, it becomes a powerful way to connect with others. Improving your speaking skills takes regular practice and a willingness to accept feedback. Every time you speak, you gain an opportunity to grow, refine your message, and boost your confidence. Over time, speaking will feel more natural, and your confidence will grow. Just remember: improvement takes patience, consistency, and a commitment to keep showing up. With dedication, you'll become a more skilled, authentic, and impactful speaker.

The Close That Drives Action

Ending your presentation on a strong note is just as vital as starting with a strong hook. A clear and inspiring conclusion leaves your audience with something to remember and act on.

One effective way to wrap up is with a call to action. Encourage your audience to apply what they've learned, reflect on their next steps, or participate in a follow-up activity. This gives your message purpose beyond the presentation.

You might also consider ending with a powerful quote that reinforces your core message. The right words, when well-timed, can stay with your audience long after your talk ends.

Lastly, sharing a personal story can leave a lasting emotional impact. It shows why the topic matters to you, builds authenticity, and creates a deeper connection with your listeners. Whether it's a quote, a story, or a call to action, closing with intention ensures your message resonates and inspires long after you've finished speaking.

To ensure your audience leaves with the right takeaway, always wrap up by summarizing your key points at the end. This reinforces the core message and gives your listeners clarity on what truly matters. Before closing, take a moment to thank your audience for their time and attention. Gratitude creates goodwill and leaves a positive impression. If time permits, invite questions or spark further discussion; this will keep the conversation going and signal that you value their engagement.

Now, let's talk about your Call to Action (CTA). Crafting a strong CTA is both an art and a science. While there's no one-size-fits-all formula, there are essential elements that can make your CTA more impactful:

1. Clarity and Specificity

Your CTA should leave no room for confusion. Use direct, action-oriented language that tells your audience exactly what to do next. Avoid vague phrases. Instead, provide clear instructions or next steps, whether it's signing up, donating, joining, or reflecting. The simpler and more precise, the better.

2. Sense of Urgency

Encourage your audience to act now rather than later. Use time-sensitive language that builds momentum, such as "Join today," "Start now," or "Don't miss out." A sense of urgency can make your message more compelling and prompt quicker action.

3. Emotional Appeal

Connect your CTA to your audience's values, desires, or challenges. Help them see how taking action benefits them personally or contributes to something they care about. When people feel emotionally invested, they're more likely to engage and follow through.

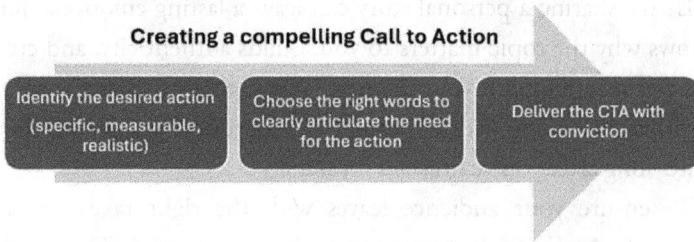

Creating a compelling Call to Action

Identify the desired action (specific, measurable, realistic)	Choose the right words to clearly articulate the need for the action	Deliver the CTA with conviction

A great speech has the power to inspire immediate action. A compelling presentation doesn't just inform. It drives change. That's why a strong call to action is essential. It bridges the gap between ideas and tangible outcomes by using clear, actionable language and measurable goals. This gives your audience a sense of purpose and a clear path forward.

Don't underestimate the power of urgency and incentives. Prompting your audience to act now creates momentum and emphasizes the importance of the moment. With a well-crafted call to action, your message can extend far beyond the stage, transforming passive listeners into active participants.

Ultimately, the impact of your speech lies in its ability to unite and empower. When we focus on shared goals and collective aspirations, we create the foundation for meaningful change. By taking action together, we can meet the needs, fulfill the hopes, and honor the desires of our teams and communities. Each of us holds the power to contribute to something greater than ourselves, and it all begins with a call to action.

Sharpen Your Edge: How to Use Feedback to Grow as a Speaker

We often excel at understanding and evaluating others, yet we rarely see ourselves as they do. This gap in self-awareness can be a significant challenge, especially when trying to anticipate what our audience truly wants to learn or take away. Bridging this gap requires honest introspection and a willingness to grow, and one of the most effective ways to do that is by seeking feedback from trusted colleagues.

Inviting outside perspectives opens the door to meaningful growth in every aspect of public speaking. Crafting a powerful presentation or keynote rarely happens in one go; it involves multiple drafts, each helping you sharpen your message, clarify your intent, and connect more deeply with your audience. These iterations aren't just revisions; they are essential steps toward becoming a more impactful, confident, and resonant speaker.

Public speaking often demands a leap of faith, requiring humility, vulnerability, and the courage to be seen. In the spirit of openness, asking for feedback is not a weakness but a strength. It is through collaboration and connection that we evolve not just as speakers, but as leaders.

By leaning into the support of trusted colleagues and nurturing meaningful working relationships, we create space for growth, authenticity, and excellence. Together, we can reach new heights both professionally and personally.

With that in mind, here are some practical ways you can start weaving feedback into your speaking journey to fuel your continued growth:

1. How to Ask for Feedback

The first step to meaningful feedback is an open mind. That means being willing to hear what didn't work as much as what did and resisting the urge to explain or defend yourself right away.

It also matters whom you ask. Choose individuals who can view your presentation from the audience's perspective, who have the experience and insight to influence and persuade, and who can offer constructive, actionable input. Ask for their thoughts on what worked and what didn't—both in your content and your delivery. Most importantly, make sure you trust their judgment and that their feedback will support your growth and help you stay aligned with your goals.

2. When to Ask for Feedback

Ask for feedback at every stage of the process. Reaching out to the same group of trusted reviewers can help you maintain consistency while uncovering new insights, without overwhelming you with conflicting opinions.

In the workplace, it's smart to seek input early, especially from your manager or peers. This not only shows that you're open to learning and improvement but also helps you catch issues before final delivery. When you thoughtfully consider and apply the suggestions you receive, you can dramatically improve the quality of your work and minimize the risk of negative feedback later on.

The key to getting helpful feedback is asking the right questions. Be specific. General requests like *"Any thoughts?"* don't always lead to useful responses. Instead, try:

- *Was the message clear?*

- *Did anything feel confusing or off-track?*

- *Did the visuals help support the point I was making?*

Getting into the details gives people something solid to respond to and helps you get feedback that's truly useful.

3. How to (and How Not to) Respond to Feedback

When you are at the receiving end of critique, practice active listening without jumping in to explain or defend yourself. Let the person finish, then ask questions if something isn't clear or you want more details. Listen with an open heart and reflect on how the feedback can enhance your speech or presentation.

See feedback as an opportunity to grow, not as personal criticism. It offers fresh perspectives, shines a light on areas for improvement, and helps you build confidence as a communicator. Practicing in environments like Toastmasters can help you get used to feedback in a supportive setting and build confidence speaking in front of others.

4. How to Evaluate and Apply Feedback

Not all feedback will be equally helpful or relevant. Sometimes it's vague, contradictory, or just doesn't fit your style or goals.

Don't blindly follow every piece of feedback you receive. Instead, evaluate it thoughtfully. Consider where it's coming from, whether it matches your objectives, and whether it's practical for you to apply. This helps you decide whether the feedback aligns with your vision and values.

Look for common themes or repeated suggestions, as they often reveal the most valuable insights. This helps you prioritize the key points and make informed decisions that support your growth and success.

When you decide what to work on, don't try to fix everything at once. Pick one or two areas to focus on, and set clear, manageable goals to track your progress. Setting specific and measurable goals for yourself will enable you to track your progress effectively.

As you work on your goals, plan how you'll practice and monitor your progress. Asking for feedback regularly along the way can help you stay on course. Trying out different techniques and approaches will also help you find what fits your style best.

And don't forget to pause and celebrate your wins. The simple act of acknowledging your progress, even the small steps, helps keep your motivation high and encourages you to keep sharpening your skills.

Reflection Questions:

Here's a checklist to help you consider the call to action, takeaways, and feedback appropriately in public speaking:

1. Call to Action

- **Clear purpose:** Have you defined a clear and actionable next step for your audience to take after the presentation?

- **Relevance:** Is your call to action directly related to the content of your presentation and audience needs?

- **Specificity:** Is the action you're asking for specific, realistic, and achievable (e.g., sign up, schedule a meeting, apply a new concept)?

- **Urgency or importance:** Have you communicated why the audience should take action now or how it benefits them?

2. Key Takeaways

- **Clear recap:** Have you briefly summarized the most important points of your presentation to reinforce the message?

- **Concise and simple:** Are the takeaways communicated in a clear and straightforward way, avoiding unnecessary complexity?

- **Audience-centered:** Are the takeaways directly relevant to the needs, interests, or goals of your audience?

- **Connection to purpose:** Do the takeaways tie back to the overall purpose of your presentation, making them meaningful?

3. Feedback

- ***Create a safe space:*** Have you made it clear to your audience that their feedback is appreciated and welcomed?

- ***Embrace feedback***: Are you open to receiving feedback, both positive and negative, to improve your skills?

- ***Non-defensive attitude:*** Are you prepared to listen without getting defensive or dismissive of constructive criticism?

- ***Evaluate actionable suggestions:*** Are you reviewing the feedback to determine what is practical and can be applied to improve your future presentations?

- ***Consistent feedback loops:*** Are you seeking feedback regularly, even after you've made improvements, to continue refining your skills?

- ***Self-reflection:*** Are you also taking time to self-assess your performance and identify areas where you can improve on your own?

- ***View it as growth:*** Do you approach feedback as a valuable opportunity for self-improvement?

Using this checklist ensures your presentation ends with impact, encourages engagement, and gives your audience clear next steps and a chance to provide meaningful feedback.

SECTION 6

LEADERSHIP BLUEPRINT:
BECOMING UNSTUCK AND UNSTOPPABLE
By Eric E. Ebron

CHAPTER 16

The 4R Blueprint: Taking Ownership of your Leadership Journey

Leadership enthusiasts are passionate people. Because of that, they naturally gravitate toward the theories and frameworks that align with their personality and style. I've always been a staunch believer that leadership isn't something granted by title. Leadership is rooted in innate human traits and abilities. We are born with the potential to lead.

History reminds us of this truth. Think of Alexander the Great, Julius Caesar, Abraham Lincoln, Mahatma Gandhi, and Nelson Mandela. These iconic figures didn't just rise to power; they shaped the course of history. We study them not only for their achievements, but for the defining moments that elevated them to leadership.

When we examine the leadership journey, we uncover pivotal transitions, and personal and professional growth, all forged through experience, skill refinement, and knowledge. It's a transformation: from uncertainty to clarity, from scattered ideas to actionable tools, and from passive identity to intentional self-development. That's how a "born leader" takes shape, not all at once, but gradually, through continuous learning and purposeful evolution.

As a kid, I unknowingly laid the foundation for this philosophy. I gathered a ragtag bunch of military brats, my friends, and formed a fledgling group called the SKA, or Stunt Kids Association. We would tear down the neighborhood roads and hills on our bikes, screaming with the kind of wild joy only kids know. Armed with nothing but a makeshift ramp of 2x4 wooden pallets and cardboard, we launched ourselves into the air, soaring over a line of kids sprawled out on the asphalt, trusting we wouldn't crush them. Cheered on by those not brave or crazy enough to join, we were the daredevils of Fort Benning, Georgia.

The next day, I'd tell them to pack lunch and snacks because we'd be gone for at least six hours. We had plans to prove our toughness. With my dad's Army bag slung over my shoulder, stuffed with rope, duct tape, assorted household fix-it items, and my lunch, we were off. We'd spend the day jumping over ditches with our bikes, falling headfirst into red clay chasms, climbing tall Georgian pine trees, and trekking through waist-high creeks that eventually led us to the Chattahoochee River.

These were our adventures, messy, bold, and character-building. Looking back, I see them for what they were: the earliest steps on a leadership path. These were the days we learned courage, grit, and improvisation. These were the moments that shaped future leaders.

Looking back on it now, some forty years later, I see I was unknowingly developing a blueprint. Beneath the scraped knees and wild stunts, there were glimpses of self-awareness, hunger for exploration, and a thirst for growth. I was already learning to navigate group dynamics, shape my own leadership style, and recognize the subtle qualities that set the front-runners apart from the rest. True leaders are driven by a relentless urge for growth and self-improvement, not as a goal, but as a way of being. For some of us, pushing boundaries isn't a choice. It's a necessity.

Decisions, Decisions, Decisions

Being proactive on your journey is at the heart of the 4R Blueprint. Whether you subscribe to the "Great Man Theory," which argues that we're born with inherent leadership traits, or "Behavioral Theory," which suggests leadership can be developed through education, experience, and practice, one truth remains: leadership is dynamic. It demands proactive development.

The 4R Blueprint bridges a critical gap between how a company forecasts your role in its 1-, 2-, and 5-year plans, and how *you*, as a leader, envision your own growth over those same timeframes. It's a framework for sustainable leadership development that empowers leaders at any stage of their journey to take ownership of their path.

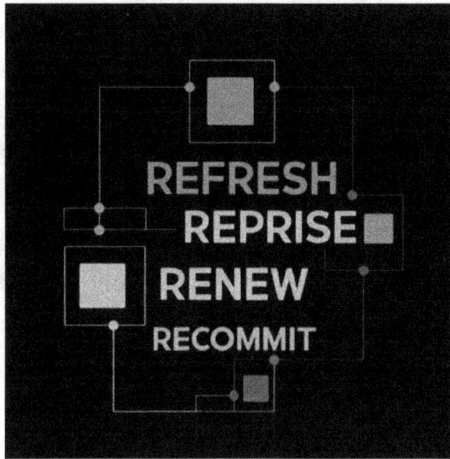

The 4R Blueprint includes four essential cycles: Refresh, Reprise, Renew, and Recommit. Each "R" helps you identify a program or pathway that moves you further along your leadership journey, something you wouldn't achieve by merely toeing the proverbial line. The blueprint propels you beyond a static mindset and into ongoing personal evolution.

Successful leaders follow the path of a marathon runner, not that of a sprinter. Like a long-distance runner, leaders must build stamina, pace themselves strategically, and endure over the long haul.

In my own career as a high-potential contributor in the aerospace industry, I experienced this firsthand. My rapid rise left behind what I call "leadership wakes," disruptive waves of change that echoed behind me. Just like a boat cutting through water, the faster you go, the more turbulent the wake. Depending on the boat's size, weight, and speed, the results can be difficult and sometimes even dangerous for others to navigate.

Dynamic leaders often feel guilty when they get the recognition and promotion they deserve. But that upward movement can create turbulence, uncertainty, instability, and disorientation within the organization. These "leadership wakes" can throw teams off balance, derail short-term initiatives, and capsize promising projects if not managed carefully.

This is where many organizations fall short. The responsibility to mitigate the impact of leadership transitions doesn't fall on the individual leader alone; it belongs to the organization as a whole. Without the right development framework, companies risk letting their best talent unintentionally disrupt the very systems they aim to strengthen.

Adaptability and Resilience

The first major challenge I faced as a leader came when the opportunity for a promotion arose. I remember watching our site leader guide senior leadership and aerospace dignitaries on tours through the facility. With ease and confidence, he highlighted our innovations, praised our people, and positioned our team as a model of excellence. He was a master at showcasing the best of what he was responsible for, and I was thoroughly impressed by this ability. It was an ability I hadn't yet developed, let alone mastered.

Then it hit me: I hadn't *adapted* to the next level. For so long, my energy had gone into proving my value, demonstrating my readiness, building the right skills, and showing both peers and senior leaders that I represented the future of leadership. But I hadn't yet embraced what it actually *meant* to operate at that level.

It never occurred to me that part of the leadership journey is about learning to adapt and bounce back, about developing resilience. So, when it was my turn to lead a group of visiting aerospace leaders around the site, I lacked the charisma and finesse my former leader had when promoting the team's achievements. That day gave me a powerful lesson: learn today what you'll need to be excellent at tomorrow.

Adaptable, resilient leaders understand how to navigate uncertainty, foster innovation and creativity, and build strong networks. These are core skills, not soft ones. The 4R Blueprint helps identify and develop those capabilities, giving leaders the tools to embrace continuous improvement and respond more swiftly to industry disruptions. When practiced, it equips leaders to seize new opportunities and neutralize threats before they take hold.

The 4R Blueprint also empowers emerging leaders to lead with new ideas, processes, and business models without fear of failure. Often, in the climb toward leadership, an intense focus on personal achievement can narrow vision. It's easy to become so preoccupied with *getting there* that we forget what it takes to *stay* there.

That's why identifying perspectives, understanding market conditions, and becoming *change agents* are paramount in being considered for future leadership growth.

Another key aspect of the 4R Blueprint is its focus on measuring the foundations of your leadership. Ask yourself:

- Are you enabling influence with those not at your direct leadership level?

- Do your peers and senior leaders see you as a strategic collaborator?

- Would your team describe you as a trusted leader in a feedback session?

Productive leaders communicate with clarity, foster alignment, and build cohesive, purpose-driven teams. These qualities separate the wheat from the chaff in today's leadership landscape.

Tortoise Versus Hare

There is an old catch-22 dilemma: How can I get the experience needed for a job offer if no one will hire me to gain the experience?

This circular logic is a real barrier for many entry-level professionals—and it echoes throughout the early stages of leadership as well. Young leaders, striving to level up, often voice the same frustration.

A similar lesson plays out in Aesop's fable, *The Tortoise and the Hare*: consistent effort and perseverance often win out over quick bursts of activity. While speed may feel impressive at first, it can breed overconfidence, complacency, and even laziness—especially when it's not backed by substance.

Leaders who rush from one milestone to the next, without truly absorbing new knowledge or visualizing how to apply it, risk becoming ineffective. Mastery requires more than achievement; it demands *intentionality*.

I remember that truth hitting me hard as a young leader, when my team grew from 65 to over 100 direct reports in just months. Suddenly, the family-like environment gave way to a complex, high-functioning shop floor. My leadership style had to evolve quickly. I needed to be nimble, responsive, and strategic, not just for my team's sake, but for the business. Senior leadership depended on it.

The 4R Blueprint reinforces the value of reviewing your past decisions—both successes and failures—to extract the tools you'll need in future challenges. This process creates a mental log for self-improvement and helps uncover patterns in your decision-making that can inform what your 'gut' will do next time. You will identify whether you are a process-oriented leader who breaks down concepts to build new instructions for your team, or an intuitive leader who can't always explain why their decisions work, but they do every time.

When you slow down the frantic race to the top or stop the unpredictable momentum that comes from poor planning, you begin to realize something crucial:

There's too much at stake to become complacent.

Every step you take with the 4R Blueprint brings you closer to your best leadership self!

The Buy-In

In project management, stakeholder buy-in is essential; it secures resources, builds collaboration, and wins advocacy from key individuals, all of which significantly boost a project's chance of success. But there's another kind of buy-in that's just as critical: the internal buy-in that fuels personal leadership development.

Just as we must persuade others of a project's value, we must also persuade ourselves that our own leadership growth is worth the effort. That takes *discipline*. Senior leaders want to know that you are who you claim to be and can deliver what you promise. If you don't believe it, it *will* show.

One of the greatest challenges I've encountered was mentoring a young leader who didn't believe in his own capability even though the results said otherwise. On the flip side, I've had to confront overly confident leaders whose flashy tactics weren't producing real productivity. In both cases, growth required an internal reckoning. Just like in change management, transformation doesn't happen without personal buy-in.

This is why the *4R Blueprint* is so powerful:

- When you *Refresh,* you realign your perspective and gain clarity on where you are and where you're going.

- When you *Reprise* past successes and failures, you mine valuable insights and strengthen your confidence in what works.

- The *Renew* phase is about pausing, reflecting, and re-energizing, as sustainable leadership requires rest and intention.

- And finally, you *Recommit* to your goals, reigniting the passion and resolve needed to keep going.

I have been asked, "Why are THESE 4Rs words important? Aren't they all kind of the same?" My answer is, "Kind of."

To *Refresh* is to restore energy that's been depleted.

To *Renew* is to rebuild something that's eroded by restoring it to its original strength or making it even better.

Stick with me, and you'll discover that implementing the 4R Blueprint is a rhythm, a cycle of repetition and restoration that equips you to grow, excel, and succeed as a leader.

When you make the 4Rs a daily, weekly, and quarterly habit, your leadership sharpens. You show up with purpose. You bring your team into clarity. You create momentum.

In Chapter 7 of my book, *Highway to Skyway Leadership: Charting a Course for Excellence in Automotive and Aerospace Leaders*, I share a personal story from 2012, when I was inspired by my Marine Corps days to take up running again. I trained diligently, building from a single mile to three, and eventually reached six. That's when I hit a wall. Pain and fatigue slowed me to a walk. For months, I felt discouraged.

Then, a coworker gave me feedback that changed everything. I adjusted my approach. After a short period of recalibration, I hit eight miles nonstop—a 33% improvement. That shift, powered by insight and accountability, made the difference between stagnation and breakthrough.

That's what the 4R Blueprint is all about:

Find what works. Stick to it. Set your pace. Respect the journey. And stay disciplined.

Leadership isn't a sprint. It's a marathon. And the 4Rs help you run it well.

Reflection Questions:

- What does "taking ownership of your leadership journey" mean to you personally?

- Can you identify a time when you felt truly "unstuck and unstoppable" in your leadership role? What factors contributed to that feeling?

- How do you currently approach continuous improvement in your leadership? What could you do differently or better?

- In what ways can embracing the "marathon" mindset, rather than the "sprint" mindset, benefit your leadership development?

Key Takeaways:

- **Leadership is a journey, not a destination.**

  Whether you believe leaders are born or made, continuous growth and development are essential for long-term success. Embrace the marathon mindset, focusing on sustained effort and consistent progress rather than quick bursts of activity.

- **Proactive development is key.**

  Don't wait for opportunities to come to you. Take ownership of your leadership development by actively seeking out challenges, learning from your experiences, and continuously refining your skills.

- **Navigate the leadership wake.**

  As you advance in your career, be mindful of the potential disruptions and imbalances that promotions can create. Develop adaptability and resilience to navigate these challenges effectively and minimize their impact on your team and the organization.

- **Embrace the 4R blueprint.**

  Utilize the Refresh, Reprise, Renew, and Recommit framework to guide your leadership development journey. Regularly assess your progress, learn from your experiences, and re-energize your passion for leadership.

CHAPTER 17

Refresh and Reprise: Looking Within and Learning from the Past

Just as runners need to know what race they are signed up for to prepare the proper training protocol, leaders on a path to success must also develop a proper training protocol. At different stages of life or career, leaders may only be required to run "5K-style" races, which are steady, predictable, and within standard corporate parameters. As long as they keep pace, they'll receive the standard acknowledgment, the standard recognition, and the standard cost-of-living increase. For many, that's what normal leadership growth looks like. In fact, when you step back and assess corporate structures, you'll notice a standard methodology used to measure both short- and long-term leadership success, one that tends to recycle the same patterns and expectations.

But out-of-the-norm leaders don't always fit that mold, nor do they try to. These individuals are like runners who move beyond the 5K crowd.

According to Livestrong.com, the most popular race in the U.S. in 2022 was the 5K, with 8.9 million participants. In comparison, only 2.1 million runners globally signed up for half-marathons. The lesson? Fewer people aim for the more demanding races. It requires more discipline, greater commitment, and deeper excitement to push beyond comfort.

Elite leaders follow the same path. They understand they exist in a crowded forest and, to stand out, they need to grow taller, dig deeper, or become more specialized. Most people, overwhelmed by their immediate surroundings, can't "see the forest for the trees."

But exceptional leaders *can*. They break through the fourth wall of leadership culture. They begin to *see the system*, recognize its patterns, and think beyond the framework. These are the leaders the *4R Blueprint* was made for.

They don't settle for standard progression.

They're hungry for more.

And they're willing to train for the marathon, not just the 5K.

Let's begin by exploring how the first two Rs—*Refresh* and *Reprise*—work in tandem to elevate leaders to the next level.

Refresh: Self-Reflection and Feedback

Growth-minded leaders regularly refresh their definition of success, drawing not just from external expectations but from within. This is the essence of the Refresh phase of the 4R Blueprint. It begins with gaining clarity about who you are and understanding what makes you valuable as a leader. These foundational insights empower you to make better decisions, build stronger relationships, and lead with authenticity.

But this is *your* responsibility, not your company's. Your leadership journey isn't something a corporate development plan can define for you. You must determine the most meaningful path forward for yourself.

Early in our careers, we often build a simple roadmap to success: move from individual contributor to team lead, then to supervisor, manager, and so on. As responsibilities grow, we're introduced to financial oversight, organizational complexity, and the political realities of middle management. But at each level, success must be redefined.

That's why the Refresh phase is essential. It's your chance to stop and ask: Who am I as a leader now? What do I stand for? Where do I want to go next?

And to answer these questions, you must engage in deliberate self-reflection.

When I think of an example of self-reflection, American author Ursula K. Le Guin comes to mind. She once reflected on the difference between interviewers who truly read her books and those who hadn't. She noted that the best interviewers, those who asked questions that made her pause and think, often left her silent for a few seconds, grappling with how to respond. She said:

"The only questions that really matter are the ones you ask yourself."

So, ask yourself:

- What skills have I mastered?

- What skills am I working on today?

- Where are my blind spots?

- What motivates me?

- Why do I want to lead?

If you're serious about advancing to the next level, now is the time to pull out your journal, sit in your thinking chair, and pause for ten seconds or more. That silence is where the clarity lives.

As a 10-year United States Marine Corps veteran, I take pride in the service that I rendered to my country. Some of my most powerful lessons in leadership came not from the teams I chose to lead, but from those I didn't choose, and yet I was still responsible for guiding toward mission success. With them, I experienced camaraderie, teamwork, triumph, and, yes, loss.

One of the hardest lessons I learned came during Marine Corps Recruit Training in Parris Island, South Carolina: how to thwart an ambush attack. You see, an ambush isn't just meant to stop or destroy; it's designed to surprise, disorient, and harass. The standard instinct in an ambush is to duck and cover. But not in the Marines. We were trained to turn toward the fire and attack with overwhelming force. No hesitation. No second-guessing. We yelled, advanced, and unleashed fury. That is what Marines do.

But to do that, we first had to know who we were. We had to understand what made us the world's most elite fighting force.

For leaders, the same level of clarity is required. During the Refresh phase, self-assessment and 360-degree feedback play that vital role. You must uncover your blind spots, understand your internal weaknesses, and reconnect with what drives you.

This is how we rise: through clarity, awareness, and action.

Reprise: Mining the Gold from Your Experiences

As you journey through life, you pick up skills, tips, tricks, strategies, and tools all along the way, some from moments of triumph and others from the sharp edges of failure.

The Reprise phase of the 4R Blueprint is about reflecting on those pivotal experiences, the "Cha-Ching" moments, where insight is earned and wisdom is forged. Sometimes these moments come with applause. Other times, they arrive disguised as pain, frustration, or embarrassment. But all of them are valuable. When you look back, you'll often uncover times when you were surprisingly sharp, so much so that you couldn't replicate the brilliance if you tried.

One such story from my career perfectly captures this.

In the early 2000s, just after the Y2K buzz, I was an ambitious individual contributor with aspirations of becoming a computer information systems guru. I sensed companies were still riding the wave of tech paranoia and saw an opportunity for me to stand out. I poured myself into training programs, collected every possible hardware configuration, and ultimately constructed a sophisticated home network: six PCs, one Apple, and two Linux machines, all linked with the latest Novell Netware management software package.

Before the drywall even went up, I had CAT5 cabling run throughout the walls of my new M/I home so I could strategically place machines across all three floors. I had been planning this for months while the construction was going on. This was my playground, my proving ground. The project tasks were completed during the final implementation, the systems were adequately configured, and the computer systems were 'go.'

Here is where things went awry: once everything was live, I couldn't help but run "what-if" scenarios to test the resilience of my system. I imagined sophisticated cyberattacks and then implemented complex security policies and permissions to counter them. I worked for 36 hours straight, refining and defending my network like a fortress.

Finally satisfied with my changes, I went to bed. The next day, after returning from my day job, I checked my work only to discover I had done such a great job that I had completely and thoroughly locked myself out of every computer and network system in my house. Determined to prove I could outsmart myself, I did just that. That humbling moment taught me a lesson I never forgot: you must recognize, reflect on, and document your patterns of success and failure. Without doing so, you risk repeating the same mistakes or failing to replicate your wins.

The Reprise phase is about developing your professional toolbox, the very tools that will carry you from supervisor to manager, from manager to senior manager, and eventually to director and beyond.

One essential strategy at the Reprise stage is failure analysis: the intentional act of unpacking a mistake to understand what went wrong. Is it your strategy or the implementation of that strategy?

Ask yourself:

- What went wrong?

- Was the issue systemic or systematic?

- Did you have the knowledge or information?

- Can you replicate the failure?

When you break failure down into its components, you build resilience, you avoid pitfalls, and you will gain repeatable knowledge that makes you better, faster, and wiser.

Another key Reprise tool is identifying your natural leadership style. I've learned that I thrive in a structure. I'm methodical, detail-oriented, and solutions-focused. My operations reflect that, and I expect my teams to deliver complete, process-driven results.

But here's the danger: leaders who aren't aware of their natural leadership state often sow confusion. Their teams may feel lost, misdirected, or worse, distrusted. Immature leaders may do this unintentionally, but the consequences are real. When you don't take the time to reflect on your past, catalog your failures, and discover your leadership rhythm, you delay your growth and muddle the path forward.

The Reprise phase helps you avoid that trap. It challenges you to extract value from every experience, good or bad, and shape a leadership style grounded in clarity and authenticity.

Mentorship: Guiding Your Growth and Amplifying Your Impact

Finally, we must talk about mentorship. In the Reprise phase, there is no tool more powerful than learning from those who have walked the path before you or guiding others along theirs.

The late author and poet Maya Angelou once said, "Do the best you can until you know better. Then, when you know better, do better."

As a new leader, you do your best. But you don't have to wait for life to hand you experience after experience to get better. Through mentorship, you can speed up your wisdom curve. You can gain access to lived experiences, insider strategies, and real-time feedback that shape us faster and more effectively.

Whether you're being mentored or mentoring someone else, the exchange is priceless. It adds depth to your toolbox and amplifies your impact.

Reflection Questions:

- When was the last time you engaged in deep self-reflection on your leadership strengths and weaknesses? What did you learn?

- Think about a significant leadership success you have experienced. What specific strategies or actions contributed to that success? How can you apply those lessons to future situations?

- Recall a leadership challenge or setback you've faced. What did you learn from that experience, and how did it shape your approach to leadership?

- Who are the mentors or role models who have influenced your leadership journey? What valuable lessons or insights have you gained from them?

Key Takeaways:

- **Self-reflection is essential.**

  Take the time to refresh your perspective and gain clarity about your strengths, weaknesses, motivations, and blind spots. Honest self-assessment is crucial for authentic leadership and continuous growth.

- **Mine the gold from your experiences.**

  Both success and failure offer valuable lessons. Analyze your past experiences to identify patterns, extract key takeaways, and refine your leadership approach.

- **Embrace mentorship.**

  Seek out mentors who can provide guidance, support, and accelerate your development. Learning from experienced leaders can help you avoid common pitfalls and gain valuable insights.

- **Know your leadership style.**

  Understand your natural tendencies and preferences as a leader. This self-awareness will enable you to leverage your strengths, address your weaknesses, and create a leadership style that resonates with your team and drives results.

CHAPTER 18

Renew and Recommit: Setting Your Sights on the Future and Embracing Change

The final two stages of the 4R Blueprint—Renew and Recommit—are where vision meets discipline. They demand a focused mindset, intentional goal setting, and an unwavering dedication to becoming the person and leader you aspire to be.

Think of looking into the future like staring through haze and fog. You may not see everything clearly, but you can just make out the outlines of what you hope, dream, plan, and strive for. That's your vision. But to make progress, you don't just wait for the fog to lift; you set your compass and begin moving forward with planning, education, preparation, and foresight as your map. Because growth, real, meaningful growth, isn't a sprint to a finish line. It's a continuous expedition. And the further you go, the more intentional you must become about your direction.

The 4R Blueprint is about setting your sights on the horizon, embracing the inevitable currents of change, and persistently recommitting to the goals that propel you forward. Noam Chomsky, often referred to as 'the father of modern linguistics,' once said, "Optimism is a strategy for making a better future. Because unless you believe that the future can be better, it's unlikely you will step up and take responsibility for making it so. If you assume that there's no hope, you guarantee that there will be no hope."

As a young general manager, I had the opportunity to host the new vice president of service solutions for a major aerospace company. She was touring the MRO facilities, and my site was next on the list. After picking her up from the airport and walking her through our operations, we sat down in my office to discuss my annual plans and how our leadership team envisioned our role in contributing to the company's bottom line. At one point, she asked, "Where do you see yourself in the future?"

By then, I had already spent five years developing my personal roadmap, so I confidently shared my 15-year career plan, one that would take me right into retirement. She was impressed by my clarity and forethought, and I was equally struck by her recognition of my preparation.

In that moment, I thought: This is what elite leaders do. We plan for the inevitable. We plan for change. We plan for success.

Renew

Sustaining personal development is an ongoing process, one that demands active engagement, deliberate goal-setting, and an unwavering commitment to execution. Reaching milestones isn't just about checking boxes; it's about proving to yourself and those you lead that your actions align with your words. This reinforces your integrity and builds lasting trust. This is where discipline becomes your greatest asset. In leadership, it's not talent alone that defines greatness; it's the ability to stay the course, especially when faced with adversity or distraction.

The United States Marine Corps instilled in me a profound sense of discipline, empowering me to overcome insurmountable odds through sheer tenacity. With the right coaching and training, elite leaders can cultivate this same discipline and consistently follow through on their commitments.

Your journey up to this point hasn't been built on magic or luck. It's the result of hard work, intentional effort, and a series of defining moments that shaped your trajectory. The same principles apply to your future growth. Just as a ship's captain meticulously charts the course, monitors the compass, and adjusts for shifting tides, leaders must regularly revisit and reassess their personal growth goals. Growth isn't a destination; it's a dynamic process of recalibration, persistence, and purposeful direction.

Ask yourself:

- Are your goals concrete and well-defined?

- Are there any roadblocks preventing me from progressing?

- Am I communicating my progress effectively to the stakeholders?

- Am I getting the adequate support and guidance that I need to succeed?

Within the Renew phase of the 4R Blueprint, leaders are tasked with envisioning what their future looks like not in vague, aspirational terms, but in clear, strategic details. For young leaders, simply stating, "I want a promotion" lacks the specificity and direction required to fuel meaningful progress. Instead, leaders must identify the exact position they seek—the title, the responsibilities, the impact they want to make, and a realistic timetable to achieve it. Only then can impactful mentors, coaches, and accountability partners step in to support and challenge them along the way.

As an operations leader, part of my role was to build leaders and remove the barriers that stood in the way of increasing shareholder value. During a one-on-one with one of my direct reports, a leader asked me, "How can I get to the next position?" I responded, "Let's build a plan and start working toward that goal." I also clarified that, as his leader, I was willing to invest a specific number of hours per week, month, and quarter to help him reach his goal. Elite leaders must understand that you are on this journey with them and that expectations go both ways. Commitment must be mutual.

But two months later, the same leader scheduled a meeting to revisit his goal. After some reflection, he realized the role he was aiming for didn't align with his personality, family life, or long-term aspirations. The effort required tested his resolve in ways he hadn't anticipated. Instead of pushing forward blindly, he asked if I could continue to work with him as a leader, coach, and accountability partner.

This is the heart of the Renew phase: the space to pause, reflect, reassess, and realign. Maybe the original goal needs adjustment. Maybe the timeline shifts. Or maybe the destination changes entirely. All of that is okay. What matters is that you're not afraid of the conversation or the future.

The Renew phase exists to help leaders build strategies that are sustainable, meaningful, and realistic. But it only works if you're willing to do the work. No shortcuts. Just clarity, courage, and commitment.

True goal setting means going beyond wishful thinking. It requires painting a vivid picture of your desired future and making that vision tangible through measurable, trackable milestones. Identify the specific training programs, mentorship opportunities, or skill-building initiatives that will close the gap between where you are now and where you aim to be. Most importantly, your goals must be realistic, strategic, and aligned with your core values. That's the foundation for sustainable success and meaningful leadership growth.

Navigating Your Growth with Strategic Waypoints

To guide you on this journey of renewal and recommitment, consider these key tactics:

- **Regularly set and review goals.**

   This is your compass, providing constant direction. Just as a captain diligently reviews, coordinates, and adjusts the ship's heading, leaders must consistently assess their progress against expectations, making course corrections as needed.

- **Be specific.**

  Don't simply say, "I want to advance." Instead, declare, "I want to become the Director of Operations within the next two years," or "I want to lead a cross-functional team to launch a new product line by the end of the year."

- **Quantify and track.**

  Define the tangible steps, training programs, and mentorship connections required to reach your goals. Break down large aspirations into smaller, measurable milestones that you can track and celebrate along the way.

- **Have realistic expectations.**

  While ambitious goals are commendable, they must also be attainable. Setting unrealistic expectations can lead to frustration and discouragement. Given your current resources and capabilities, ensure your goals are challenging yet within your reach.

- **Value alignment.**

  Your goals should resonate with your beliefs and priorities. This alignment minimizes unnecessary stress and ensures that your pursuit of growth is fulfilling and meaningful.

- **Set clear deadlines.**

  Establish target dates and checkpoints for monitoring your progress. Deadlines provide structure and accountability, helping you stay focused and motivated.

Young leaders can easily aim high and set bold, ambitious goals like becoming a vice president without fully understanding the steps required to get there. But skipping over the foundational work, the skill-building, and the strategic positioning often leads to years of frustration and stalled growth.

Leaders must recognize that there is a method of advancement. Leadership isn't a leap; it's a climb, taken one deliberate step at a time. You don't go from an entry-level to the executive suite overnight. You reach the summit by following a clear path marked by strategic waypoints such as education, experience, opportunity, and timing. Each must align for the ascent to succeed. The key now is to align yourself with the right blueprint and have the discipline to see the program through.

The Power of Small Wins

Another strategy taught within the Renew phase of the 4R Blueprint is the Identification of quick wins within your existing goals to grow momentum and build motivation. When we pinpoint smaller milestones and celebrate the team's achievements, we allow confidence to seep down into the mindset of high-performing team members! No matter how small, these victories create a sense of progress, invigorate your team, and reinforce the value of persistent effort. This strategy is particularly crucial for emerging leaders who need to see the tangible impact of their contributions to build confidence and solidify their leadership identity.

Entrusted with a new team, I undertook a challenging project early in my career. We faced many obstacles and setbacks, but I consciously focused on building their confidence and showing them they were as good as any team they had seen in the department. I meticulously broke down the project into smaller, more manageable tasks.

We achieved a significant milestone within thirty days, exceeding our initial expectations. I publicly acknowledged the team's hard work and celebrated our success. This small win boosted team morale and established my credibility as a leader who could deliver results, even in the face of adversity. A few of those original team members have gone on to lead teams, becoming operational leaders themselves and continuing the principles instilled in them by that initial team.

Lastly, elite leaders should reanalyze previous failed plans and decisions. This analysis involves a dynamic, ongoing review of these decisions, as close to real-time as possible. Regardless of experience or expertise, every leader will inevitably face challenges and setbacks. The key is to view these not as failures but as invaluable learning opportunities. Use these moments to teach yourself how to pivot, to adapt, and to refine your approach. Analyze what went wrong, adjust your strategies, and show the resilience and discipline that inspire confidence in your ability to lead and excel.

Recommit: Ownership and Accountability

Elite leaders understand that critical decisions should never be made in a vacuum. Senior leaders embrace this fundamental truth and recognize that true accountability includes acknowledging their role in both success and failure. You cannot accurately assess what went wrong without examining how you contributed to the process.

A clear indicator of immature leadership is the belief that all suggestions and decisions you make should lead to success. That mindset is not only unrealistic; it's dangerous. Leadership is not about being infallible; it's about being responsible and accountable. Leaders who operate in isolation often avoid accountability, but elite leaders actively seek wise counsel, coaching, and collaboration to make the best decisions for both their teams and the organization.

Growth, in any form, requires energy. Just as living organisms need nourishment, teams need purpose to thrive. When your team understands the 'why' behind your goals and connects with the purpose driving your efforts, they begin to experience shared ownership. When you articulate your vision and invite them into it, you light a collective fire. Passion grows. Momentum builds. Obstacles become challenges to conquer, not barriers to success.

The "Yeah, But..." Moment

I once poured my heart and soul into revitalizing a team that was floundering, plagued by low morale, lack of direction, and fractured cohesion. Together, we put in the hard work. We addressed the root issues, aligned our goals, and reignited our shared purpose. Eventually, we achieved extraordinary results that far surpassed what anyone thought possible.

But after all that progress, one team member dismissed it with a shrug and a simple, "Yeah, but that was going to happen, anyway."

I'll be honest, it stung. In that moment, I felt the sting of having my leadership effort minimized. I had leaned into the hard work, acknowledged the issues, engaged the team, and helped build a culture of commitment and excellence. Our success wasn't luck; it was leadership. It was intentional. And while the comment frustrated me, it also reminded me of a truth all seasoned leaders must hold onto.

Success doesn't always receive the recognition it deserves, but that doesn't make it any less real. Focusing on the overall impact and celebrating the journey, regardless of individual perspectives, is crucial in leadership.

After that moment, I took the team member aside and walked through multiple change management models together. We carefully reviewed how our strategies aligned with best practices and how our deliberate actions led to success. By engaging him directly and transparently, I was able to improve his opinion by 10%. It wasn't a full turnaround, but it was progress, and progress is what leadership is all about.

Change is the only constant in the ever-evolving business landscape. The most successful leaders are not just those who accept change; they are the ones who embrace it, adapt their strategies proactively, and demonstrate unwavering commitment to the company's mission and vision. This adaptability fuels growth, inspires teams, and ensures sustained success even when the road gets tough.

The 4R Blueprint: A Roadmap to Thriving

The 4R Blueprint, with its interconnected stages, serves as a compass, guiding you and those you lead toward sustainable personal and professional growth:

- **Refresh** your perspective to gain clarity on where you stand and map out a clear path forward.

- **Reprise** past experiences to extract invaluable lessons, building on what works and avoiding the pitfalls of yesterday's mistakes.

- **Renew** your commitment through strategic goal setting, empowering yourself to pause, reflect, and recharge throughout the journey.

- **Recommit** to your goals to reinforce discipline and fuel the drive needed to achieve extraordinary outcomes.

As a leader, your commitment to personal growth profoundly affects those you lead. If you resist growth and evolution, you risk limiting not only your potential but also that of your entire team. Seek mentors and role models, leaders who walked your path and emerged stronger. Attend summits, absorb their insights, and internalize their wisdom. Commit to becoming the best version of yourself, not just for your own sake, but for the benefit of those you have the honor of leading.

Remember, the leadership journey is a marathon, not a sprint. The 4R Blueprint is your roadmap to thriving in this ever-changing landscape.

Reflection Questions:

- What are your current leadership goals? Are they specific, measurable, attainable, relevant, and time-bound?

- How do you stay motivated and maintain momentum when working towards challenging leadership goals?

- Describe a time when you had to adapt your leadership approach to embrace change. What did you learn from that experience?

- How do you connect with the "why" behind your leadership goals? How do you keep your passion for leadership alive?

Key Takeaways:

- **Embrace optimism.**

  Cultivate a positive outlook and believe in a better future. Optimism fuels motivation, drives progress, and empowers you to take responsibility for creating the future you envision.

- **Set clear and ambitious goals.**

  Define specific, measurable, achievable, relevant, and time-bound (SMART) goals for your personal and professional development. Regularly review and adjust your goals as needed to ensure they remain aligned with your values and aspirations.

- **Take ownership of your development.**

  Don't wait for others to provide opportunities or guidance. Proactively seek challenges, learn from your experiences, and continuously refine your skills and knowledge.

- **Recommit to your growth.**

  The journey of leadership is ongoing. Regularly re-energize your passion, recommit to your goals, and maintain unwavering dedication to your personal and professional development. Embrace change, adapt your strategies, and persevere through challenges.

CONCLUSION

Your Career, Your Power: It's Time to Take the Lead
By Will Lukang

Throughout this book, you've explored the key pillars of a thriving, fulfilling career: career management, emotional intelligence, stress management, networking, public speaking, and leadership. Each has equipped you with insights, tools, and frameworks to elevate your professional life. Now, it's time to bring everything together into a cohesive action plan—one that will empower you to step into the next chapter of your career with clarity and confidence.

Step 1: Define Your Vision and Goals

Success begins with self-awareness and intentionality. Pause and reflect on what you want to accomplish in your career. Ask yourself the following questions:

- What are you good at? What's your gift?

- What does your career mean to you as an employee or entrepreneur?

- Where do you see yourself in three to eight years?

- What skills, experience, and achievements will help you get there?

- What do you need to change to speed up your progress?

Write your career vision clearly and boldly. Set SMART goals—Specific, Measurable, Achievable, Relevant, and Time-bound—and define milestones that will help you measure your growth along the way.

Step 2: Own Your Career Growth

Your career is your responsibility. Waiting for opportunities is not a strategy, but creating them is. This book emphasizes the importance of self-leadership, ownership, continuous learning, and adaptability.

Assess your current skills and identify what you need to enhance and improve:

- Create a personal development plan and track your progress.

- Seek a mentor who can guide your growth.

- Adopt a growth mindset and embrace challenges as learning opportunities.

Step 3: Network and Build Relationships

Your network is one of your most valuable career assets. Cultivating genuine, lasting connections can open doors, spark ideas, and accelerate your progress. It is an ongoing process.

Apply the following principles to maximize the results of your networking activities:

- Take a genuine interest in getting to know others.

- Nurture your connections. Check in regularly and establish new relationships.

- Network when you have a job, not just when you need one. Like a plant, you must plant the seeds early so that when you need support, your network is already there.

Step 4: Communicate and Lead with Impact

This is one of the most overlooked aspects of career success. Technical skills might get your foot in the door, but communication and leadership will elevate you to the next level.

Improve your public speaking skills: practice, prepare, and volunteer to present your ideas. Focus on:

- Organizing your thoughts, improving your body language, and demonstrating confidence

- Mastering the art of storytelling to engage and influence your audience

Step 5: Build Resilience and Manage Stress

Success isn't just about achieving goals; it's also about sustaining performance. Managing stress and developing emotional intelligence are essential to maintaining your mental and physical well-being. Foster your mental well-being by:

- Identifying your stress triggers and learning how to manage them effectively

- Protecting your energy by setting healthy boundaries

- Developing emotional resilience to navigate workplace challenges

Step 6: Take Action and Stay Accountable

Knowledge without action is meaningless. Implement what you've learned from each section of this book and take intentional steps to manage your career effectively. Use these tactics for continuous growth:

- Commit to lifelong learning. Seek opportunities to improve your skills.

- Track your progress and hold yourself accountable for your growth.

- Celebrate your successes. Acknowledge milestones and small wins.

- Surround yourself with the right people who genuinely want you to succeed.

- Join a mastermind group and continue evolving into a better version of yourself.

The seeds of success have been planted, and you're now equipped with the insights, tools, and clarity necessary to take your career to the next level. It's time to nurture them with focus, intention, and an open heart.

Take charge of your path.

Apply what you've learned.

Embrace the leader you were born to become.

Your future is waiting.

Let's go.

YOUR EXCLUSIVE READER BONUS: CAREER BREAKTHROUGH MASTERCLASS

Congratulations on taking the first step toward unlocking your full career potential by investing in *Career Breakthrough Playbook: Get Unstuck, Get Ahead*.

As a thank you for being a valued reader, you now have exclusive access to the Career Breakthrough Masterclass — a high-impact training designed to help you apply the strategies, frameworks, and tools from this book in real life so you can move from insight to action even faster.

In this Masterclass, you will:

✔ Clarify your career vision and set achievable, measurable goals

✔ Build a personal development plan tailored to your unique strengths

✔ Overcome career plateaus with proven breakthrough strategies

✔ Learn how to leverage mentors, networks, and storytelling for growth

✔ Create an actionable timeline to accelerate your progress

How to Access Your Masterclass:

1. Scan the QR Code below to verify your purchase.

2. Follow the quick sign-up process to secure your spot.

3. Get instant access to masterclass videos, and community.

📌 Important: This offer is available only to readers of this book. It's our way of making sure you get maximum value and results from what you've learned.

Your career breakthrough starts now — don't just read the playbook, put it into play!

SCAN ME

ABOUT THE AUTHORS

WILL LUKANG

Will Lukang is a change agent, award-winning author, seasoned C-suite executive, international speaker, coach, and trainer, passionate about leadership development and executive coaching. His colleagues and clients know him as an intuitive, professional, skilled presenter who can build high-performing teams and consistently deliver innovative solutions and cost-effective results.

Nurturing talent in other people is Will's number one priority because he believes the true measure of a leader is how well they serve others. The cornerstone of his servant leadership practice is the concept of leading by example, a value instilled in him by his father. He believes we can make a more significant impact by acting with others rather than alone because we can achieve incredible things with the proper support, motivation, and mission. Regardless of our position, title, or degree, finding and bringing out the best in others helps us bring out the best in ourselves.

Will released the award-winning book *The Seeds of Leadership* in 2024, where he leveraged his leadership experience and advanced education in leadership coaching. Earlier in 2012, he co-authored *The Character-Based Leader*. He frequently designs and delivers practical training and powerful presentations for corporations and teams focused on organizational development and talent management.

HIBA TANVIR

Hiba Tanvir is a certified emotional intelligence (EI) practitioner, speaker, and consultant who helps leaders and organizations harness emotional intelligence as a competitive advantage. As the founder and CEO of HT Compassion, she equips teams with tools to build emotional resilience, reduce turnover, and foster thriving workplace cultures.

With an MBA and advanced certifications from Harvard University and the Gottman Institute, Hiba blends strategic business acumen with deep emotional intelligence expertise. She has been invited to speak at CEO and HR summits, the North Texas Information Security and Systems Association, and the Speaking Consulting Network in Rhode Island—where her energizing sessions have sparked real change across industries.

Her global initiatives include the Man Up youth program in Nigeria, the English and Emotions series for refugee families, and Hope Kitchen—a social enterprise providing dignified work for women through home-based catering. Her work has been featured in *The Dallas Morning News*, *Voice of America,* and *Inspired Generosity.*

Hiba champions EI as the real intelligence in today's AI-driven world—and a proactive solution to the mental health crisis. Known for her interactive approach, she leads hands-on workshops using Play-Doh as her favorite tool to drive engagement, creativity, and team connection. Learn more at www.htcompassion.com

DONYA SMIDA

Donya Smida is a certified coach, hypnotist, and international speaker specializing in stress management and leadership. With 17 years of corporate experience, she transitioned from a high-level executive role, overseeing a $100M portfolio and 30+ employees, to full-time coaching, training, and speaking.

Donya has been featured in *TED-Ed* and *Madame Figaro* and on other notable platforms, spreading the message that stress can be managed and that professionals can thrive without compromising well-being. She delivers impactful talks on leadership, stress management, and performance, guiding entrepreneurs and managers to reduce stress, gain clarity, and increase efficiency.

Donya's mission is to help busy professionals overcome stress, reclaim their time, and lead with confidence. Her journey from corporate pressure to personal empowerment fuels her passion for helping others create a life of success without burnout. She is a wife and mom of three: Elyes, Shams, and Jad.

JOËL VUADENS-CHAN

Joël Vuadens-Chan has 36 years of corporate experience across various industries (banking, aviation, IT, insurance, and education). Before founding the Swiss Leaders Group, a global leadership/communication and sales development group for global corporations, his last corporate position was as a Sales Director and member of the Executive Board member at an insurance company in Switzerland.

In addition to building his own business and career and investing his time pro bono in the development of others, he was appointed National Transformation Coordinator of Equip Leadership. He has supported several non-profit organizations in Switzerland, the UK, and Malaysia, his wife's home country.

An award-winning leader, he is passionate about coaching leaders and their teams to function in a connected, creative, efficient and value-added manner to their stakeholders. He is known for his highly ethical cross-cultural relationships and his ability to acquire new skills and communicate them enthusiastically.

A panel and webinar host and guest on several international platforms, including the WEF extended conference in Davos, he is also a university guest lecturer, trainer, and a public speaker worldwide for organizations such as MIT Professional Education, Regent's University London, and Swiss Business School.

NEHA DESHPANDE

Neha Deshpande is a multifaceted professional whose journey is as inspiring as it is diverse. An Agile enthusiast, TEDx speaker, international author, mentor, and trainer, Neha has carved a niche in the professional community. Her passion for Agile methodologies is reflected in her work, driving efficiency, innovation, and transformation. A sought-after speaker, she shares insights on leadership and growth at global platforms like TEDx.

Neha is deeply committed to continuous learning. As an active Toastmaster, she has refined her communication and leadership skills, earning accolades for her impactful presence. Her problem-solving acumen, calm demeanor, and signature smile make her a trusted and admired leader. Her motto, "When life gives you lemons, enjoy the lemonade," reflects her positive outlook.

Her creative journey includes roles as an editor, poet, author, and show director. As editor of *WO-BRIGHT* magazine and co-author of *Let's Trance and Aashayein anthologies*, Neha brings a graceful voice to human emotions and storytelling. Her writing reflects depth and sensitivity.

Neha holds an engineering degree from COEP, Pune. Married to Maneesh for 15 years, she treasures time with their two daughters. A visionary leader and creative soul, Neha beautifully balances her thriving career and fulfilling personal life.

ERIC E. EBRON

Eric E. Ebron is a distinguished operational leader and leadership expert, renowned for delivering measurable wins. Drawing on a decade of service in the Marines and a successful career leading in the aerospace industry, Eric knows what it takes to build high-performing teams and navigate complex organizational changes. He is dedicated to helping leaders apply the discipline, adaptability, and strategic thinking honed in demanding environments to achieve significant success.

As the best-selling author of *Highway to Skyway Leadership*, Eric champions a transformative approach to leadership development through his innovative 4R Blueprint system. This empowers leaders, consultants, and trainers to accelerate their careers, expand their influence, and become sought-after innovators. As founder of Eric E. Ebron Consulting, Eric focuses on helping professionals find their ideal position to drive success in competitive industries. He holds an MBA from Friends University and a bachelor's degree from The Ohio State University and is a frequent guest on the *Lead Forward* podcast.

ACKNOWLEDGMENTS

From Will Lukang

This book is the result of collective wisdom, shared experience, and a shared passion for helping others unlock their full potential.

I extend my deepest gratitude to my fellow co-authors—Neha Deshpande, Eric E. Ebron, Donya Smida, Hiba Tanvir, and Joël Vuadens-Chan—for your insight, dedication, and unwavering commitment to this project. Your unique perspectives and contributions have enriched every page and brought this vision to life.

Thank you for your collaboration, your stories, and your belief in the power of career transformation. It has been an honor to walk this journey with each of you.

Together, we created something truly meaningful—and I couldn't be more grateful.

To my daughters, Faith and Maddy—thank you for inspiring me to grow and be better every single day. You are both the light and driving force behind everything I do.

To my wife, Jane—thank you for your unwavering support, your steady belief in me, and your constant words of encouragement. I am truly grateful for your love and partnership.

From Hiba Tanvir

To my mother, Shamsa Tanvir—who taught me the power of having a vision, the value of a meaningful career, and the joy of never losing the zest for soaring.

To Papa, Sabiha, Zozo, and Enjee—thank you for pouring your unconditional love and support into me.

To my tribe of women—you know who you are. You have lifted, anchored, and championed me in ways words cannot fully capture.

And to my sons, Izyaan and Zaraan—you are my daily inspiration to become the best version of myself. May you grow up to be men of deep character, gratitude and lasting impact. May you always use your strength, privilege and voice to uplift those around you.

From Donya Smida

To my family, who patiently stood by me while I poured my heart into this work.

To my clients, who inspire me every single day with their courage, resilience, and willingness to grow.

To my mentors, who reminded me to dream big and to never shrink myself. And to myself for not giving up, for rising after every doubt, and for choosing courage over comfort.

AND to you, Will, thank you for your confidence and support.

From Joël Vuadens-Chan

To my beloved wife, Olivia, whose unwavering love and support inspire and empower me every day. To my sons, Timothy and Ethan, who are my joy and my inspiration through their hunger to learn and grow, and often to challenge me. So blessed by all three of them.

From Neha Deshpande

To my ever-supportive husband, Maneesh, whose heartfelt appreciation and pertinent feedback cultivate the accuracy and wholesomeness in everything I do! To my daughters, Mahika and Shamika, who are my guiding light and constant motivation — their creativity and passion drive me to learn new things and find joy in the smallest moments of life!

I feel so fortunate to have you all in my life! Thank you for always being there!

From Eric E. Ebron

To my dearest wife, Sandra, your belief in me, demonstrated through your consistent and thoughtful actions, has been a constant source of strength.

To my wonderful children, Marion, Terrance, Keora, Alyxus, and Jadé, thank you for the unique ways you have shaped me as a father. Watching you grow into compassionate and capable individuals has been one of the greatest privileges of my life. Your perspectives, your challenges, and your triumphs have broadened my understanding of leadership and empathy in profound ways. Thank you for helping me see the world through new eyes and for continually inspiring me to grow.

www.ingramcontent.com/pod-product-compliance
Lightning Source LLC
Chambersburg PA
CBHW071600210326
41597CB00019B/3336